# DISCONNECT, REVERSAL, And RESTORATION

## Gaining God's Power and Provision for Your Life's Mission

Dr. Robert and Annette Stagmer

Scriptures quoted are New King James Version unless otherwise specified.

# Table of Contents

# PART THREE
## REVERSING CRISIS THROUGH COVENANT RESTORATION

# PART FOUR
## REMOVING BLOCKADES TO YOUR FUTURE

## Preface

The commandments of God establish the boundaries of our relationship. Within the relationship boundaries, we are assured of His faithfulness to keep His covenant. Without the boundaries, we can also be assured that the curse will be present. Within the boundaries is peace, but without is chaos.

*"I beseech you, therefore, brethren . . ."* Paul begins the urgent message of Romans 12 by pleading with the believers to move into a new dimension of their Christian walk. He is so concerned with the urgency of this word that he humbles himself to plead with the believers to heed the words of the Lord that he's been given. In Hebrews five and six, the writer chides the Hebrew believers with the expectation that by now, they should be teachers but are still in need of learning the basics.

We feel like Paul in that we most earnestly desire for you to consider the message that we have been commissioned by the Lord to bring to you. The *Disconnect, Reversal, and Restoration* message is of such an urgent nature that without this understanding, you may not be prepared to deal with the circumstances that you will soon face. This is not necessarily new content, as much as a clarified application of the truths you have already been taught.

Putting in place your clarified Kingdom message, a consistent discipleship process, and preparation to deal with the mass of broken people that is about to descend on every body of believers, has to be our utmost priority.

This message will impart life and momentum. Please don't miss this urgent preparation for the harvest.

*A renewed mind thinks the thoughts that God intended to be thought.*

# ENDORSMENTS

The Stagmers have done it again, presenting us with a gift of clear revelation. You will draw closer to God as the scales fall off your eyes from years of misinformation and tradition. They describe how prophets and apostles work together to bring both realization and actualization. They also clearly explain Cessationism and the roots of that lie. And you will understand the importance of your personal mission statement. This book draws the response, "Yeah, I knew that, but I could never put it into words." That's what the Stagmers have done for us over the past 18 years – put words to our vague concepts. Robert and Annette mentored and taught us to be more of the ambassadors God called us to be, giving us confidence to step out with more faith and more courage. This book will do that for you also. As they say, "It's all about staying near to God and moving forward."

Randy & Barbara Walter[i]
Shiloh Ministries, Berlin, Maryland

In *Disconnect, Reversal, and Restoration,* Robert and Annette Stagmer peel back layers and layers of Judeo-Christian history to get at the core concept of the faith: the Kingdom of God as it was meant to be lived. Through an encounter with the living God and a personal "mission statement" downloaded by the Holy Spirit, a person can actually climb into the "driver's seat" of life and prosper in ministry. As the author says: "the aroma that you produce when you are walking in a Kingdom way is so attractive it draws people in." The mustard seed of our life is programed for a fullness of a predetermined outcome while you experience the Shalom of God (nothing missing, nothing broken, and nothing out of order). As a published author myself, I heartily invite you to take the journey with Robert and Annette.

Dr. Scott T. Kelso, General Overseer, Five Points-Greater Columbus Apostolic Network
Chairman, Charismatic Leaders Fellowship

# ACKNOWLEDGEMENTS

To Dr. Jon Ruthven for inspiration; Yvonne Barr for content advise and technical assistance; to all our fellow ministers for prayer and guidance

# INTRODUCTION

In this book we will demonstrate the cause and effect of the current dilemma and power vacuum in much of the present day Christian church body. We will show what happens when the church becomes disconnected from the power of God. Reversing the Order of God's instructions, results in violation of covenant. When covenant is violated, the result is the benefits of covenant are no longer available to the violating party(s).

Unfortunately, all sin has corporate consequence. So we all suffer when sin abounds in the collective. God is so concerned with covenant between man and Himself that He initiated the necessary restoration. An examination of the workings of the religious and political spirit reveals how they cooperate to cripple the power, authority, and unity of the body. We will show how restoration of covenant restores the power and authority to each individual and the collective body of Christ. Finally, this book reveals how mission and covenant are directly connected with God's supply.

# Shalom also means that <u>the origin of chaos is destroyed!</u>

# PART ONE

# THE GREAT DISCONNECT

Acts 1:4 - 4 And being assembled together with them, He commanded them not to depart from Jerusalem, but to wait for the Promise of the Father which, He said "you have heard from Me; for John truly baptized with water, but you shall be baptized with the Holy Spirit not many days from now."

# CHAPTER 1

## THE ABSENCE OF POWER

### What was God's original intent?

In 2005 we were in a conference in Texas with Apostle/Prophet Chuck Pierce. At the end of the conference, as we were leaving, Chuck called out to us: "Robert and Annette, when you get back to Maryland, start calling yourself Apostles." That scared us! We thought if we did that, people would think we had lost our minds. Since that time, we have witnessed God establishing us in an apostolic gifting to the church as He is doing with many leaders across the globe. After several years, we perceived that we were indeed apostles.

The basis of this teaching is to see the power that God intended to be in the church, restored. Through man's reasoning that led to false doctrine, the power of miracles, signs, and wonders has been held hostage. The power of the church is cut off at the source. That's why we call this *The Great Disconnect*.

What do we mean when we discuss the glory of the Lord? We must answer this question. The restoration of the presence of the glory comes through the presence of God. Creation was filled with glory; then sin came. With sin, came the loss of God's presence and a resulting loss of God's glory and power. We know the story. Jesus came to model and instruct, to redeem mankind, and pave the way to restore power.

The perception of the glory is growing. We hear God. We feel God. We understand things we didn't understand. We connect with people. The supernatural breaks out. Things we're praying about come to pass. This is what we signed up for, isn't it? The more we see it, God's Kingdom is starting to appear here and there. We want to move forward. It's all about staying near to God and moving forward.

Some of us don't like change. Some of our personality types don't like it, others do (the impetuous ones, like Peter) and run out ahead of everything before they get all of the instructions. That's not so good. We need to think about change and be ready to accept it when the timing is right. This present moment is a time of change. This is an era of change for everybody. It doesn't matter whether you want to change, things are going to change around you.

We need to know how to get on board and go with the Wind of God. Know this, God says in Isaiah nine, "Of the increase of His government and peace there will be no end." Of the increase of His government and *peace,* there will be no end. *Peace* is usually left out: His government and <u>peace</u> shall increase. *Shalom.* What do we know about the meaning of *Shalom*? Peace. But beyond that it means nothing broken, nothing missing, nothing lacking and nothing out of order. Shalom also means that the origin of chaos is destroyed. How surprised we were to find out that Shalom had greater meaning than we had thought. As long as we could remember, we had thought that Shalom had just meant hello, good bye, or peace. We never realized that there was a fuller meaning. The expanded clarification brings new revelation of the usage of that one word.

New Apostles are arising. The New Apostolic Reformation[2] is here. Whether you like it or not, there are big changes happening. These changes are often not popular but necessary.

Little changes are easier because they don't make people shift. Make a little tweak here and, suddenly, it's like a trip to the chiropractor. You get one little thing out of order and you are in pain. Snap that in, and everything works. Everything's empowered. Now you can do mighty feats. Before, you couldn't do anything; you couldn't even move a minute before that adjustment took place.

Apostles deal with the big picture; they see things and make big tweaks. They tell what they see coming up ahead because they deal prophetically and are linked with the prophets in the restoration of the government of God. That's how Ephesians 4:11 works.

*¹¹ And He Himself gave some to be apostles, some prophets, some evangelists, and some pastors and teachers, ¹² for the equipping of the saints for the work of ministry, for the [e]edifying of the body of Christ, ¹³ till we all come to the unity of the faith and of the knowledge of the Son of God, to a perfect man, to the measure of the stature of the fullness of Christ; ¹⁴ that we should no longer be children, tossed to and fro and carried about with every wind of doctrine, by the trickery of men, in the cunning craftiness of deceitful plotting, ¹⁵ but, speaking the truth in love, may grow up in all things into Him who is the head—Christ— ¹⁶ from whom the whole body, joined and knit together by what every joint supplies, according to the effective working by which every part does its share, causes growth of the body for the edifying of itself in love.*

Without the prophet, the apostle may not see what is coming in the distance. They need to work together for both visualization and actualization. That is the pattern Jesus set forth: First Apostles, then prophets, evangelists, pastors and teachers. These are the gifts (gift persons) that Jesus gave to His church for the purpose of equipping the saints. It is the saints who are to do the ministry of reaching the world and establishing the church, that His Kingdom would be seen in the earth (even in our generation).

**What did Jesus preach? How did He preach it?**

Just take a look at how Jesus did it. He had a little group of followers. He picked the twelve out of the crowd. What did He do? He went out specifically, got the twelve, taught by example and demonstrated the power. The twelve and others were equipped and sent out. Right before Jesus returned to heaven, He told them to go to Jerusalem and wait. Since He ascended on the fortieth day after resurrection, we know that they had to wait ten days for the descent of the Holy Spirit. They did not know how long they would have to wait because they had not known it would happen on Pentecost. This was the anniversary of the giving of the law on Mt. Sinai.

When Holy Spirit came with tongues of fire and strange languages, they were surprised like everyone else. They had been obedient to wait expectantly. Filled with fire and power, the apostles rose up in leadership of the church on that very day. Their leadership was apostolic. Jesus only prepared, empowered, and raised up apostles. He did not designate other of His followers as prophets, evangelists, teachers and pastors. He worked only with apostles. Later when they recognized someone was a prophet, it was the apostles who confirmed their calling. The prophets then were linked with the apostles, and would tell them what they were hearing from God. They talked about it together. All New Testament prophets were apostolic prophets-Kingdom building prophets.

The prophets speak what they are seeing and hearing, but the apostles are given the implementation as that is their special gift to the body. Prophets who operate disconnected from Apostles will seldom achieve God's intent and may even run into trouble and rejection. Apostles who fail to recognize the benefit of the prophetic, will likely fall short of God's full intent.

To know the time and the season, in the Old Testament, was a gift given to the tribe of Issachar. The New Testament apostles make the plan, and get it out to the rest of the body. This is how we implement the prophetic word and direction.

The glory is always better when God restores apostolic order. That is because it's more like it was in the beginning when Jesus set up His church-His ecclesia. The Bible says, in Ephesians four, that when He ascended, Christ gave gifts, (more accurately gift persons), to the body of Christ; all of the gift persons. There were and are, those who said that all the apostles and prophets died out. That is not so. There have always been apostles and prophets in the church. They just haven't been recognized as such. That wasn't the plan of God. As He restores these things as they were meant to be, we all come up into a higher place "in the glory" (the revelation of Himself in His body on earth). We understand and see and hear more clearly as the glory is restored.

In this era of change into which we now enter, "things are coming into greater order." It will begin looking somewhat different. Remember that ninety-three percent of creation is <u>invisible</u>. You cannot see it. But is it real? Germs, invisible gases and all kinds of things are in this 93%. Seven percent we see, and ninety-three percent we don't. Those who say, "Show me, I'll believe that when I see it," are in real trouble.

Number one, there's just not any faith in that statement. Secondly, you are going to be in trouble at a time when you need to have grown in your faith and know how to exercise it. That is what God tells us in His Word. He wants us to grow in faith. Jesus said, "When I return, will I find faith upon the earth?" [3] He wants you to study to show yourself approved unto God, because you will need greater faith for the time we are now entering. When faith increases, we can move in the supernatural. Do you know that the ability to walk on water was already in Peter? He just had to exercise his faith and ask God if he could do it. Jesus said, "Yes…" So Peter believed it and he walked. He could do it because it was already <u>in him</u>. It wasn't a "Shazam". It's in you! Many things that you have never experienced are already <u>in you</u>. All you need to do is learn to get in better shape in your **faith zone**. Jesus did not use power that is not already available to us. He was here to show us how to live in God's original intent while destroying the works of the devil.[4]

God wants us to grow from precept to precept; line on line, we go upward like steps. He doesn't have us skip them, because then we won't know how we got there or be able to explain, teach, or demonstrate it to anyone else. Its line upon line, and up we climb. Everything will be about going up in the coming years; remember that. The glory that you see now in some churches, you've never experienced so greatly before, have you?

Let me tell you a story that really happened. I (Robert) was asked to speak at a funeral in a Catholic Church. The message was very evangelistic and full of Holy Ghost fire. I was concerned that I might not be well received in that church. When I got there, I met the priest in charge. To my utter surprise, the priest was someone I had known for a long time. Not only that, he was baptized in the Holy Spirit and moved strongly in Holy Spirit power. When I got up to speak, he was sitting behind the altar praying for me and the presence of God was in that place. As I spoke I heard several people gasping and even pointing to the altar. The altar was lit by the Shekinah Glory of God in that place. There was such an anointing of power, everyone felt it. A daughter of the deceased man, who had not been following God, rededicated her life to the Lord. Several others were refreshed in their faith that day.

There will be other changes for the good. If God makes any changes, it's just going to be more glorious. He never gives you less. You don't go from glory to less than glory in God's plan. So just go with what God is doing here, there, everywhere. Be encouraged.

We'd like you to write down three words: *witness, disciple,* and *Kingdom.* We believe in the upcoming seasons, these will be the most important concepts that you can grasp and they will come into play in such a way that you will be called upon to participate. So, let's be ready.

We would like to recall to you the prophecy given by a prophet in June 2013. Now we've known that prophet since 2002 and even before that, we had followed the things that he has said. We know the accuracy and completeness of the words that he gives. He gives them carefully, sometimes having held on to them for 15 years or more before he speaks them. Sometimes these type of prophetic words are hard to understand. It's easy to read things into these words that are not there.

As we understood it, part of the prophecy said there would be an event such that it will be seen across the country and everyone would know that it is God. When it happened it would kick off a revival; a harvest for six months like the world has never seen. It would start on the east coast and sweep across the nation. Now, what does that mean to us? Well it means several things. First of all, if it happens as prophesied, that's wonderful and if it doesn't and it happens at some later date that's wonderful; if it doesn't happen exactly that way that's wonderful too because we see perfectly and imperfectly. (*We see in a glass darkly*) [5]

We believed that there was going to be such an event, but it didn't happen that way. In fact, I (Robert) was wrong about the timing of the event but not about the implication of such a happening. We needed to be prepared just the same as if it were going to happen. What do we need to be prepared to do? We need to be prepared to witness our faith in such a way that people, who have no background whatsoever in Christianity or the bible, can hear the gospel clearly. Secondly, we need to disciple those people that will come in.

Recently, we were talking about the Billy Graham crusade foundation and how they've done studies and found that **less than 25%** of the people who made the altar calls are now attending churches or are active Christians. Less than 25%! We were involved in the 1980 Billy Graham crusade in Baltimore. We know the degree to which follow-up was done. We know how hard we worked to follow up on those who made commitments. For us to hear that only 25% of those people are still active Christians, cuts us deeply and says we somewhere missed it badly.

We are going to explain to you why we missed it and what we can do about it. Our discipleship process must improve and must get on a basis where those people who make decisions are retained. In addition to that, we must all be prepared servants. We should all be at the level of serving one another, serving in the body, listening to the Lord and to the pastors. "How may I serve?" Listening to their guidance, all should be prepared to lead small groups; one person, two people, whatever. Then go up a step, a step of glory, maybe up two steps, or maybe three. You are going to be the core workers in the vineyard when the new believers come. Get ready. God says He's preparing you so you'll be ready. At whatever level, you will be ready. When the great harvest begins, you are going to be inundated with brand new people. If you are not prepared to lead, these new ones will rise up and lead. They will not know what they are doing, as they have not the maturity.

The best leaders are those who are walking in maturity. I ask this question, when we were talking about the five-fold gifts, "Which gift makes the best leader?" Is it the leader with the developed, mature gift that knows who he is, who the other people are, and can put the people in the right place to use their gifting for the right purpose? Yes. A mature leader knows how to draw gifts out of them. No one should be doing everything; if they are, they're doing a one man show. That's a demonstration of an immature leader.

Jesus gave gifts to the church to prepare the members to fulfill a mission.

*And He Himself gave some to be apostles, some prophets, some evangelists, and some pastors and teachers,* **12** *for the equipping of the saints for the work of ministry, for the [e]edifying of the body of Christ.*
**Ephesians 4:11**

The job of these gift persons is to prepare the saints for the work of ministry. All the saints are to minister not just the professional clergy.

*We must be prepared to preach the Kingdom, disciple new believers, and deal with broken people!*

# CHAPTER 2

# WHAT IS THE MOST IMPORTANT CONCEPT IN SCRIPTURE?

## The Core Concept

What would you say is the most important concept in all of scripture? Discipleship? If you were Jewish what would you say? The Law. There are different opinions throughout the bible-believing world as to what is the central concept of the Bible.

What was the central mission of Jesus? Was it the cross? Was it the resurrection? Perhaps it was the commissioning of the apostles or destroying the works of the devil? All of these things are important.

What did Jesus preach? He preached the Kingdom, the Kingdom of God. What is **the Kingdom message** and how did He preach it? He preached it with parables and with power. Why did He use parables? He said it wasn't for everybody, it was for a select group. Your mind had to be *in the process of redemption* for a parable to make sense.

> *He replied, "Because the knowledge of the secrets of the Kingdom of heaven has been given to you, but not to them.* [12] *Whoever has will be given more, and they will have an abundance. Whoever does not have, even what they have will be taken from them.* [13] *This is why I speak to them in parables: "Though seeing, they do not see; though hearing, they do not hear or understand.* [14] *In them is fulfilled the prophecy of Isaiah: "'You will be ever hearing but never*

*understanding; you will be ever seeing but never perceiving.*[15] *For this people's heart has become calloused; they hardly hear with their ears, and they have closed their eyes. Otherwise they might see with their eyes, hear with their ears, understand with their hearts and turn, and I would heal them.*
Matthew 13:11-15

To implement the parables, there was power. Jesus exercised power with love, but He spoke to the situation directly. Did He ever ask the Father to do anything in that respect? The only time in scripture that Jesus asked the Father specifically to do anything is when He said, "If it be possible let this cup pass from me." **He spoke to things.** What did He teach His disciples to do? Think of Peter and John at the Gate Beautiful with the lame man. Peter said, "*What I do have, I give to you. In the name of Jesus, WALK!*" (Acts 3:6). What did Peter and John have? They demonstrated the power, authority and love of Jesus.

## Central theme

The central theme of the scriptures is the relationship between God and Man. God created us and told us how to live. Man then sinned, so we needed a written teaching to guide us. Even that did not restore the perfection that God created. So He made a covenant with us.

> "*Behold, the days come, saith the Lord, when I will make a New Covenant with the house of Israel and with the house of Judah: Not according to the covenant that I made with their*

*fathers in the day when I took them by the hand to lead them out of the land of Egypt; because they continued not in my covenant, and I regarded them not, saith the Lord. For this is the covenant that I will make with the house of Israel after those days, saith the Lord; I will put my laws into their mind, and write them in their hearts: and I will be to them a God, and they shall be to me a people: And they shall not teach every man his neighbor, and every man his brother, saying, know the Lord: for all shall know me, from the least to the greatest. For I will be merciful to their unrighteousness, and their sins and their iniquities will I remember no more.* (Jer. 31:31-34.)

Now clarify that for a moment. God made a covenant with the people of Israel. Why did He do this? Why did He choose Israel? Why did He make a covenant with them particularly? It was because of Abraham. Abraham believed what God promised and his faith in God was accounted unto him righteousness. God made a covenant with Abraham's descendants: first Isaac, then Jacob whom God called Israel. Was there a covenant before that? Yes. There was a covenant in the Garden of Eden. Then there was the Abrahamic covenant, and next was a Mosaic covenant. We do have a history of God making successive covenants. Now He comes to a need to restore His chosen people and He prophesies through the prophet Jeremiah, that there is going to be a New Covenant.[6] It will be different, because the covenant of the law was external. Now God is saying that the law, the nature that I want you to demonstrate, is going to be within you. It's not an external set of rules anymore. We can rule out the law as the central theme of the Bible, as now we have a new covenant. How was this new covenant to come about?

*Jesus preached the Kingdom through beatitudes, parables, and by demonstration.*

# CHAPTER 3

# THE DISCONNECT

## Church Practice Vs Scripture

The problem exists that at the time of reformation, the reformers, Luther, Calvin, and others, were trying to correct what they saw as error in the Roman Catholic Church. Their original intent was not to break off and be a new denomination. Their original intent was to correct the abhorrent practices. The Ninety-Five Theses centers on abuses in the church. The number one thing that Luther saw in error was the selling of indulgences. The Pope was charging money in order to get deceased relatives released from purgatory. He was charging money for getting them into heaven. That made the congregants, if you will, consumers, purchasers of religious services. God never set it up that way. As a young student, Luther traveled to many places to study. At one point in his life, he was a monastic monk. Before Luther actually came back to Germany, he was in Italy at the Vatican. He saw how richly and how flagrantly money was spent. He saw that even in the monasteries, they were living in luxury. Not only was the fact that they were rich, but their life-style was lavish while the poor suffered and starved!

Luther had been objecting to this before he posted the Ninety-Five Theses. Remember that he was a professor, a doctor of theology in the Catholic

Faith at the University of Wittenberg. By posting the Ninety-Five Theses on the door of the chapel, he said, "I see these things and I want to discuss them". That's all he really did. That was a practice of scholars. It wasn't an unusual thing. It was usual for scholars to post their questions. What was a bit unusual was the number of theses posted – ninety-five of them! His wording was accusatory of the Pope. Instead of the Pope writing back to him, or sending someone to debate him, they took offense. All the cardinals and the Pope took offense and immediately condemned Luther, saying, get rid of him, he is a trouble maker. They did not treat him like the scholar that he was.

That's quite a story. The agitation that existed between the reformers and the formal Catholic Church developed into a who-said-what and the reformers came up with "Sola Scriptura". You know what that means - only the scriptures. In other words, we're not going to accept anything unless it's clear and provable from the scriptures. Then **the reformers** went about saying there were things that used to happen that don't happen anymore. Because they couldn't see things happening anymore, they searched through scriptures to prove it and they really went far out trying to prove it and never really did. They said, the apostles have passed away. We don't see apostles in the church anymore, we don't see prophets in the church anymore, we don't see the gift of healing in the church, we don't see miracles anymore, and <u>because</u> we don't see them now, we're going to develop a theology around that. That theology today is called **Cessationism**. If you have not heard that term before, please write it down. Over the years, we have met many **cessationists**. I (Robert) was raised in the Methodist Church, which at the time was not necessarily cessationist, but which simply did not have miracles going on. Methodism had seen miracles, signs, and wonders since its founding. But they sort of passed away after the 1920s. They passed out of the church. The church that I attended was a very large, wealthy, and ornate Methodist church, very much into liturgy. We just never heard about miracles happening now and didn't know that there were contemporary miracles. We never heard the negative side, nor did we hear the positive side. When I was baptized in the Holy Spirit, I immediately saw that all of this was possible; I didn't have any negative teaching flowing through me.

When we became involved in the Christian School movement, we met some very traditional, hardline, fundamentalist Christians. They had the strangest theology. They were strict about scripture and about everything. They took every single thing as absolute yet they did not accept miracles. They didn't accept apostles. We used to have great talks about it. Fortunately, my contact was a man who would talk about it and not get angry. Many of them would get extremely angry. We just thought, okay they just don't have the Baptism of the Holy Spirit. They haven't figured it out yet, but someday they'll get baptized in the Holy Spirit and they'll change their minds. That was just the way we thought. Then we met some very strict Lutherans and also some very strict Presbyterians. Over the years, we started meeting these different people and they all seemed to think the same way. We were really perplexed by the fact that they all thought the same way. They were different denominations and yet they all had the same thought pattern. It came from **the reformers** because they were rejecting the authority of the Roman Catholic Church.

It's what we call, "THE GREAT DISCONNECT". They disconnected. There was a deliberate decision to disconnect. What's the problem when we have disconnection? There is no power; no light. This protestant tradition of rejection of miracles was, in fact, **a misstatement of the mission and message of Jesus**. The gospel of traditional Protestantism, cut off the authority and the power of the true message of the real gospel. They did it to undercut papal authority. The Catholics said this: "We have miracles to prove our doctrine, where are your miracles"? The Protestants said, "They are false miracles, they don't prove anything".

Proof and demonstration are two different approaches. Proof says, "Here is my basis, now I will show you why it is correct." Demonstration shows you, then explains what was shown. When miracles accompany the presentation of the Kingdom, there is immediate attention and curiosity.

*...because they didn't see Apostles in the church, or prophets, or healing, or miracles, they developed a theology around what they didn't see.*

*That theology today is*

# Cessationism.

This protestant tradition of rejection of miracles was, in fact, _a misstatement of the mission and message of Jesus._

# CHAPTER 4

## A NEW COVENANT

### Understanding the Purpose of Holy Spirit Gifts of Revelation and Power

We must understand the purpose of the Holy Spirit gifts of revelation and power. If you believe the cessationist way, all miracles ceased. The purpose of the Holy Spirit gifts is **to put demonstration power in the preaching of the Gospel of the Kingdom**. If you are a cessationist, you can't even have prophesy because there can't be any prophets. All you can have is what is written in the Bible. Nothing else will be revealed. I guess they didn't read the Book of Revelation, of which parts have not happened and there's much yet to be revealed in the texts, step by step. A central characteristic of the New Covenant was to understand the gifts of the Holy Spirit, through which power came. Even though the apostles had already been out healing and casting out demons throughout those three years with the Lord, Jesus said (paraphrased) "I don't want you going out. You wait in Jerusalem until the Holy Spirit, the promised one, comes upon you and then you'll have power to minister." They waited, the one hundred twenty waited in the Upper Room until the Holy Spirit came.

We need to understand the purpose of the Holy Spirit gifts of revelation and power. When we have those gifts available to us, we don't speak just words, we speak into the spirit of the individual. Words penetrate the mind, the thinking power. But words that are inspired and come with power and revelation, speak into the spirit.

Faisel Malick, a former follower of Islam, is now a Christian pastor, speaker, and writer.[7] He speaks about going to Christian meetings and how he had Christianity all figured out. Because he was a business man, his plan was to follow someone who was successful and do what they did. He saw how successful the Christians were in getting people saved and coming to the Lord. He thought he could do the same thing for Islam. He could just use the same tactics. But essentially, when he tried it, the Holy Spirit grabbed him, and he ended up going to the altar and accepting Jesus. Before that happened to him, he was angry with the people when they went up to make the altar call. There were thousands there. He kept being given a front row seat. So, he went up as a good Moslem to argue the point, because they like to argue about Islam. He got pressed by throngs of people coming to give their life to the Lord. He'd be pressed so he couldn't ever get to the man with whom he wanted to talk. Every time he'd go forward again, the press came and he got really angry. The Lord said, "These are my children". He said, "I'm your child". The Lord said, "No, these are my children". He kept saying "these". He had said it three times before

Faisal got the revelation. He committed his life to Jesus and he became one of the children.

The central characteristic of the new covenant is that the word is written on your mind and on your heart! As you speak forth with revelation, then you speak into the heart and into the mind and a change takes place. You cannot speak revelation to an unbeliever and they not be affected. They may not make a commitment right at the moment but they are affected by it. What was the purpose of the cross – redemption! Jesus paid for our sins. That part is certain. Did the cross complete the restoration on its own? Did Jesus dying on the cross do it all? Jesus dying on the cross was like the opening of a door that purchased the right to become sons and daughters, the process of God's intended restoration.

> *"Yet to all who did receive him, to those who believed in his name, He gave the **right to become** children of God."* (John 1:12) NIV

It was like the beginning of setting things into motion, so that a series of events could occur that would usher in the New Covenant. He had to descend into hell. He had to ascend into heaven and be glorified. But each event takes you through an expanded doorway. The cross was like the doorway. As each event triggered the next event, the power was released. Consider His commissioning of the disciples. He commissioned the disciples before the

Holy Spirit fell. He commissioned them and then the Holy Spirit fell on them. He'd given them the authority to do mighty works. When the Spirit fell upon them, that authority became explosive! Traditional protestant theology significantly distorts the Christian message and the work of Jesus. **It disempowered the New Testament witness**.

I loved Billy Graham and I loved what he did, but I look back at that process of bringing those people to the altar. We encouraged people to bring someone and then stay with that person and disciple them. We were not to say anything about the Holy Spirit Baptism or power. Converts without a partner were referred to a local church to follow up. Many of the churches did not do a thorough job. Most of those that did, stopped at the salvation message. New believers were not really discipled nor told that there was more to come, i.e. more power. There was **a disconnect**. Their commitment didn't last in many cases.

This is why people fell away. It's true of almost any large crusade. If there's not good follow-up, if there's not a good discipling process that follows it, then you will lose those people. They are going to float back into the life they were living beforehand. **If you have a disempowered theology, you will disciple others to be disempowered**.

You will be nice people that bring your money into church, show up, be quiet, be talked to, and then leave. Is that all there is to Christian life? Are you empowered, released, and envisioned to go forth and do the works of Jesus? Are you disempowered or disconnected?

## The Disempowered, Disconnected Message

The message that we heard growing up in both the Methodist and Catholic Churches, and the message that was continually preached for a long time was that there was a cost of expunging sin. Jesus paid the price and if you took communion regularly, and asked forgiveness for your sins, your sin could be expunged. You could be free. They told us that salvation was free, but you have to continually be doing this process. If you stayed good after that, then you'd go to heaven. That was essentially the gospel that was being brought forth. There was little or no message of a relationship with God. There was no mention of a new life in Jesus or any empowerment for being a Christian.

Wesley articulated the four pillars: scripture, tradition, experience, and reason. He did not divorce faith from reason. Tradition, experience, and reason, however, are subject always to scripture, which is primary.[8]

If you were Catholic, you had the Baltimore Catechism in 1st grade. Why did God make you? It is to know Him, to love Him, to serve Him, and be happy with Him in heaven. What happened to life? What about that? Just be good and you'll go to heaven. That is the general concept even in most churches today. Is that all there is to the Gospel? How many of you, after you were born-again, actually didn't have that revelation yet and you were still trying to get people to do this and that? I (Annette) was a supreme "do this" person. So, I really appreciate finding out that He's done it.

## Sola Scriptura vs Cessation

I didn't know there was a <u>doctrine of cessation</u> taught in most seminaries; did you know? They not only don't understand that Jesus intended us to have the power and gifts of the Holy Spirit, they literally <u>teach against it</u>. **Cessationism** states that there are no apostles or prophets, although somehow or another, pastors, teachers, and evangelists still exist. They teach that there's no new revelation. That really bothers me. There's no new understanding, it's all given, so you can't develop in your spiritual knowledge. All that is based upon the Bible to be perfect as it is and that nothing can be added to it. (I'm not advocating adding anything to scripture.) In this regimen, there is nothing to be learned that has not already been taught in the scriptures. However, the seminaries teach and use the teaching of Bible expositors. If you can't add to the scriptures, how can you study someone's interpretation?

After having studied the bible for nearly 50 years, we can still pick it up any day and get something new out of it. You will never come to the end of your understanding the scriptures. You will never come to your ending of piecing scriptures together into a new and more vital picture. I am not advocating taking scripture out of context. I am saying that there is room for greater understanding. Cessationists are stuck with what is written in The Word, except when it's convenient to reason their way past it. Then they leave *sola scriptura* and bring in all sorts of other proofs. But it only happens in a denial kind of way. Cessationists deny what is in scripture when it doesn't fit their paradigm; when it doesn't happen in a revelation kind of way. As they ignore the gifts of the Holy Spirit, they trump *sola scriptura*!

What was the Protestant version of the Catholic? The mass is based on the Passover. I believe that. I believe that when we say communion, we enter into the continuum of God's revelation and presence, and we go all the way from the ram in the bush to the lamb on the altar.

**Clergy** – Not based on the Melchizedek priesthood
**Scripture** – Can be explained only by Clergy

Clergy, as it is constituted in most denominations, is a copy of the Levitical priesthood. According to the scriptures, in the New Testament, there is a priesthood of believers. In the Protestant and in the Roman Catholic Church, you have to be ordained into a specific priesthood. An Episcopal priest, told me, that we need both the Melchizedek and the Levitical, because if we don't have the Levitical, how can we do the liturgy? How can we do the liturgy? They had to reinvent authoritative positions, when Jesus already set His authority into the gifts to the church, working together (Eph. 4). The apostles were not up at the top like they were in the Roman concept. No. Apostles and prophets are servants and they are what the body is built upon. This is the picture that the Lord gave us and it bears it out in the word of God. Having a separated out clergy means there is hierarchy. There are the leaders and there are followers. That is the doctrine of the Nicolaitans.[9] Jesus did not set it up that way.

Somebody had to be left in charge or there would be everyone doing what was right in their own eyes. (Judges 21:25) When no one is in charge there is chaos. We know what that produced from the Old Testament. Jesus gave us these governance gift persons. The Apostles set things in order, but were not heavy handed. The whole idea was empowerment, so that <u>everyone was able to grow up to the full maturity</u>[10]of their level of gifting and were released to do it. No one was holding them back. The early church was not limited by power struggles and finance issues.

As time passed, new rules were made to protect those in power positions. Schisms occurred over territory and interpretations. It got so bad that believers were not allowed to have scripture, even scrolls. If you were caught with the scriptures, the penalty was severe. Whatever you needed to know, you were just to show up at church and you would be told what you needed to know. You didn't need to know that much! That kept you in spiritual bondage and the exalted leaders in the place of power.

The establishing of the clergy is not scriptural and is totally different than the gifts of apostles, prophets, evangelists, teachers, and pastors which Jesus gave to the Church when He ascended (Eph. 4); totally different. The fact is, when you create a clergy that says that the rank and file have to go through the clergy to get their understanding of scripture and to communicate with God, you have left Jesus' original intent for His church. That is the practice of the Nicolaitans. Jesus warns the church that following the Nicolaitans could cause the church to lose its lampstand.[11]

**The doctrine of Cessationism changes the structure of Jesus' church**. It is not just wrong, it is downright dangerous. You really need to grasp that, because we didn't grasp it until recently. It makes the laity the paying consumers of religious information and services. You know it, you can see it and you have been it. We need to present the Kingdom as a charismatic expression of love, miracles, signs and wonders.[12] We have gone out together in the market places and put this into action. What was the one comment from some Christians that totally stunned us? "We didn't know Christians could do things like this." That's what they said. Not in just one case, every time we went out that's what Christians that we met, blessed, and prayed for, said. They said, "I think I can do this". We said, "We think you can too." "Well, I'm going to go home and tell some of my friends". "Yes, do that", we affirmed.

## Mission of Jesus

What was the central mission of Jesus? To make disciples out of you and me. What is a disciple? A disciple is somebody that follows the master. The cross was the necessary step to initiate the new covenant. Scripture affirms the New Covenant promise (see Jeremiah 31:31-34) of a charismatic spirit of prophesy and power bestowed on those who believe in Jesus. If you want scripture for that you can look at Rev. 19.

## A Counter Movement to Cessationism

The Biblical Theology Movement, which is a counter movement to Cessationism, sought to allow the bible to speak with its own voice. They were sola scriptura too, but they were sticking to the scriptures. They are certainly a correction to Cessationism; however, the cessationists don't accept it. Who is the most well-known cessationist in the United States? John McArthur is known as California's great bible teacher except he vehemently comes against the gifts of the Spirit! So much so, that when Randy Clark had The Voice of the Apostles meeting in Florida, John McArthur intentionally scheduled a meeting right there, advertising Randy's meeting as "Wildfire". He preached against Global Awakening. It's not wildfire, but it is fire, great fire. If you read your bible, God is described as being great fire by the prophet Ezekiel in chapter one.

Throughout history, those who have denied miracles, signs, and wonders, did not try to do them, as they did not see them happen; so they said they were not legitimate. That was because they did not see them. The Holy Spirit comes with revelation, prophecy and power. We know that. Jesus specifically criticized the theologians of His day by saying,

> **"You know neither the scriptures nor the power of God" Matt 22:29**.

That's not the Jesus Church. Revelation characterizes the new covenant spirit. (Jer. 31:33 and Isa. 59:21) Jesus continued saying,

> *"The very works that I do—bear witness of Me, that the Father has sent Me. [37] And the Father Himself, who sent Me, has testified of Me. You have neither heard His voice at any time, nor seen His form. [38] But you do not have His word abiding in you, because whom He sent, Him you do not believe.[39] You search the Scriptures, for in them you think you have eternal life; and these are they which testify of Me."* (John 5:36-39)

The Theologians of His day weren't prepared in anyway. They didn't have the baptism of John the Baptist. He went out preparing the way, so the people could see Jesus was the Messiah when He arrived. When He arrived they didn't get it, because they weren't prepared. The immediate revelation takes place in the heart. It takes place by the Spirit, John 14:26 and 2 Cor. 3, also in Heb. 12. Immediate revelation is the very covenant that represented Jesus' "sent from" mission. The immediate revelation, He showed with **miracles**, **signs** and **wonders**; He modeled them. Next, He commissioned others to do them. He bestows them on us to continue His mission. Everyone knows that the mission statement of Jesus is Isaiah 61. That is what He commissioned the Apostles to do, and they understood it. The disciples discipled others and that's what their mission was and when it gets down to us, it's our mission statement. You have to be prepared and empowered to go and do it or you can't fulfill the **Great Commission**.

> *"Remember, I will put my law in their minds and write it on their hearts and I will be their God and they shall be my people.* (Jeremiah 31: 33)

Where do you think He did that? When did He do that? That was **Pentecost**, one of God's commanded feasts. (Lev.23) Thousands of Jews from other nations were there in Jerusalem. That was the birthday of the giving of the law, when it was written on stone. Jesus chose that day, of course, to reveal the greater plan God had for the future which was the giving of Holy Spirit with fire and power. John the Baptist told his disciples that the one coming after him (Jesus) would baptize with Holy Spirit. (John 1:33)

## A New Covenant - A New Priesthood

When did Jesus get His power? It followed His being baptized in water and with the Holy Spirit. Holy

Spirit descended on Him in the form of a dove. We believe Jesus, in humility, went down into the river to receive water baptism. There's nothing wrong with believing that, it's true. But what else happened when the Holy Spirit came upon Jesus? Did Abba Father show up? "Yes" and the Father spoke. The Son was standing there. **The Holy Trinity witnessed this important event.** Where else is that in all of scripture? John says, *"You ought to be baptizing me, what am I doing here baptizing you?"* Jesus says, *"Well, let it be for righteousness sake".* [13] And we all think that's what it says. The bible isn't written originally in English, is it? One of the substitutions for *righteousness* would be <u>in right order</u>, <u>in right standing</u>. **Do it so we can get into the right order.** For those who studied and really were the studiers of the law, they knew if they went back and read in Leviticus 21, they would find that when a new High Priest came in, there was an order to be followed. The High Priest was washed (mikvaed) (Hebrew) before he got the new identity put on him. It was right there, that Jesus became the new High Priest of the Melchizedek order! (Hebrews 8)

The outgoing High Priest washed the new High Priest in water- a Mikvah. John the Baptist was of the Aaronic Bloodline through his mother, Elizabeth, (Luke 1:15) and his father as well. He was filled with Holy Spirit in the womb. He was called in the spirit and power of Elijah; therefore, he was also a prophet.

He was to ready a people, prepared for the Lord (Luke 1:17). Being also thirty years old, he would have become eligible to serve as the Levitical High Priest. Here is where the priesthood changes. John was the pivotal link between the old and the new priesthood. No more the Levitical Priesthood. Here begins the Melchizedek Priesthood with a new eternal high priest from the tribe of Judah (Hebrews 8:13).

It is true. Jesus was empowered there. Next, He went out into the desert, led by Holy Spirit. He had to go through a lot of testing. We grew up thinking well, it was different for Jesus. He was Jesus. He was Jesus yet He never played the God-card. He wants you to know that you can do anything that He did. Anything is possible for those who believe, for those who follow the prompting of Holy Spirit. Jesus said you had to live a fasted life to get rid of some things. If you want to be like Jesus, there's a price to pay. He wasn't like everyone else, you know. He spent His day in a different way.

That is what we say about the importance of Pentecost. **It's not an option.** You know that is how it has been presented many times to people. Yes, you were born again. That is wonderful; but would Jesus have required the apostles to go and wait to be baptized in the Holy Spirit if this baptism in the Holy Spirit was not something that they needed to build His Kingdom?

> *"...**Do not leave Jerusalem**, but <u>wait for the gift</u> my Father promised, which you have heard me speak about. For John baptized with water, but in a few days* **<u>you will be baptized with the Holy Spirit</u>**." (Acts 1:4-5)

If Jesus, the Son of God, needed to have Holy Spirit come upon Him to carry out His mission, whom do we think we are to consider this as an option?

"Well, I don't think I'll have any of praying in tongues. I don't like that." We have had it said to us. People that were baptized in the Holy Spirit, but didn't want to prophesy or pray in tongues, abandoned the gifts because it made them seem strange. They act as if the gifts are a smorgasbord at a Sunday dinner, going down the serving table and having a little helping of this and passing that by, saying "No thanks".

The truth is, we are down to the wire. We are preparing for the King to come. He is coming soon; whether that's 10 years or 20 years or more. Some of us may be here to see it. We have a lot of work to do. It is the time of joining with the heavenly hosts to war. Hear what God is saying, then declaring it. We are declaring that a new era is here. It is a time when the veil between heaven and earth is becoming thinner. It is possible you can have a new identity along with Holy Spirit's empowerment before time, you can pull in your new identity and you will get all of the graces and all of the revelation that is already implanted in you. It will come and you will see how to proceed. It is not for you so you can say, **"I'm this or I'm that"**. No. It is to empower us to bring in the harvest. It is to affect more people. We need to bring in the full harvest. To accomplish this, people need to see us in a different identity; that of heaven's ambassadors.

God knows what the next step is. You know there's a scripture for this too, Zechariah 3. This is where the angels came and they took the dirty robes off of Joshua. They washed him and clothed him with robes of a new identity, putting a clean turban on his head. This meant he would be speaking in a new pure and holy way.

God is ready to do this for all who can see themselves clothed in their ambassadorial identity. It is because we need it; the Kingdom mission needs it.

**Let us pray**: "Lord, we are seeking whatever You have for us. We are not seeking it for us, but for Your Kingdom and Your great pleasure, Lord. We would that not one should perish but everyone should come to a full, mature understanding and participation in Your Kingdom in our lifetime. Lord, we need a new washing, we need the clean turban. We need an immediate thing to happen, by your great glory. Lift us up to your banqueting table. We can't reach up as high as we need, Lord. We need a boost, a help. Help. Hear us, Lord. We want to be effective disciples. We ask this in Jesus' name. Now we reach up and by faith, we pull it down, Lord, for ourselves. Lord, we thank you. We thank you. We ask now for empowering angels to be sent from your throne for each person. Not the guardian angels, that are already ours, because your word says they are forever before your throne. That's a good thing. Thank You. Keep them praying for us, Lord. But by the way, give us a fresh anointing Lord, one that will empower us to do that which hasn't been done. This new identity as heaven's ambassadors would cause people coming into our presence, to experience the fear of God and they would say, "What must I do to be saved?" Lord, from the holiness of your throne, give us ministering angels. Thank You, Lord, for hearing our prayer." Amen.

All believers have been given the responsibility and authority by Jesus Christ to rule and reign on this earth, not as despots, but as servant leaders. Jesus would say, "You know you've got my mind on it, now declare it."

*"You shall declare a thing and it shall be done for you."*     (Job 22:28)

We should declare every day that the veils are being taken off the minds of the people of our city, state, and nation. This speaks of those people with whom we will come into contact with on the job, call out their names, your children, your grandchildren, and your family members. Do this whenever Holy Spirit reminds you. You do not have to memorize exact words. These people have a veil on- you want if off.

*"Veil, be removed from their eyes."* (2 Cor. 4:4)

Jesus is the truth. Spirit of truth, come to these who need you, who live now in darkness. Open their spiritual eyes to the light of life in Jesus." Amen.

*If we are to be Kingdom builders, the Baptism in the Holy Spirit is **not** an option.*

*If you have a **disempowered theology**, <u>you will disciple others to be disempowered</u>.*

All believers have been given the responsibility and authority by Jesus Christ to rule and reign on this earth, not as despots, but as _servant leaders._

# PART TWO


# THE GREAT REVERSAL

My simplistic way of thinking says that Post-modernism and Cultural Marxism are the result of reversing the Greatest commandment with the second. Making first second and second first, results in seeing God through man's eyes rather than seeing man thru God's. The effect is to reject authority and introduce chaos into the application of a system of governance.

# CHAPTER 5

# MISSION OF THE CHURCH

**Our mission is to inject the seven mountains of culture with righteousness and Kingdom principles such that we cause a Niagara of reversal, repentance, and revival that leads to reformation and transformation.**

An article was written by Dr. John Ruthven.[14] Dr. Ruthven is professor emeritus of Theology at Regent's University. He was also the architect of the Randy Clark Scholar's program. Sitting under Dr. Ruthven is an experience. It is a total mind changer in the depth of understanding. Dr. Ruthven is the author of What's Wrong with Protestant Theology and On the Cessation of the Charismata. His premise in the article is that the whole Bible comes together when God fulfills His promise to establish a new covenant, where the law is written on our mind and our hearts. The mission of Jesus was not simply the cross (we are not diminishing the cross or the work of salvation, but saying there is more to it). It was paving the way for what was promised in Jer. 31:31. The cross and the sacrifice of Jesus was necessary; the necessary shedding of blood to ratify the covenant, the necessary cleansing of sin which had to happen before the new covenant could be established in our hearts and in our minds. The sending of the Holy Spirit was the **essential part** of empowering us to receive that covenant. Dr. Ruthven concluded, in this particular article, that the baptism in the Holy Spirit was not a "goody" added on to salvation, but was part and parcel of who Christ had commissioned us to be and what He had commissioned us to do. We could not fulfill the Great Commission; we could not fulfill what Christ had put in us to do, without the Baptism in the Holy Spirit. He went on to prove that belief theologically, historically, and biblically. It was from that article that we developed the teaching called <u>The Great Disconnect</u>.

It was also probably, I can't directly connect this, what opened our minds and hearts at our 2017 conference in August, where Holy Spirit really hit us in the midst of where we were without our expectation. I (Robert) began my fifty slide presentation and I got through five slides and that was it. I never got any further. It wasn't the teaching, or the preaching that did it. It was Holy Spirit in our midst. Annette and I went home and the next week we were still in awe, and I said to her, "How would you describe what happened"? This is what the Lord gave her. He said, "One seamless garment." She continued, "It was more than just the words 'One seamless garment'. When you have a seamless garment, no human hands have made it. When He said that, there was an impartation. You could taste the word, you could feel it. It was a holy touch that He did to unify. He put us on like a garment. He made us one. Amazing!"

From that, we went forth riding throughout the state of Maryland with Randy and Barbara Walter and others on the <u>One Seamless Garment Prayer Tour</u>. We went to every courthouse, in the 24 counties of the state of Maryland and Baltimore City. We stood on the steps and we declared that justice and righteousness are the foundation of our God's throne. (Ps.89:14)We were tired of injustice and unrighteousness in government. It's time for servant leadership everywhere. We evicted the enemy and all his plans that have taken their seats in governments everywhere, up to the State Capitol and on beyond into Washington. We began seeing differences as soon as we did that. The local newspapers carried the stories of three state legislators who were unseated due to corruption. The reason we do all these journeys is so you can hear everyone's strategies that they've tried and which have worked. This is strategic, governmental intercession of the ecclesia-*"...the people who know their God shall be strong and do exploits"*. (Daniel 11:32)ASV. We can get all of these things done together and clean up our governments. *"The earth is the Lords, the fullness thereof, the world and they that dwell therein."* Ps 124:1 KJV

"The Great Reversal", the Lord said back in January. Following the direction of Holy Spirit, we got our notebooks and read the notes from the past 8 or 9 years. Going through them, there was a note from 2008 in which **prophet Chuck Pierce said there was coming a divine reversal**. That was 2008! Then at the beginning of 2018, the Lord said,

"The Great Reversal". We started seeking Him and He revealed some things to both of us. We knew that we were supposed to go forward into the depths of the whole matter. Calling all of our conference speakers we said, "What will the Lord say to you on this subject?" We believe if we're intentional in our listening and intentional in our application of what we hear, there will be a divine reversal. It will first be in Jerusalem, then in Judea and into the uttermost parts of the earth, as you take it forward from here. It is going to happen everywhere. Jesus said first, that He was the light of the world, but after a while He said what, *"Now are you the light of the world"* (Matthew 5:14-16, Philippians 2:15). It's time for us to shine.

Let us look at the church, speaking of the broad spectrum of the body of Christ. We look at the great efforts that many, many pastors are making to try and reach out to the cities; yet, we see a disconnect. Real unity of purpose is just not happening and we wonder why with all this effort and all the concern, things really have not jelled the way they should. It occurred to us that no one has been in agreement with exactly what the church is supposed to do. There is a dichotomy between lack of clarity, and a competition, if you will, between the various groups and churches. Many have not laid down their territorial claims, so that they can literally cross the line between one denomination and another. We proposed about a year ago that a university which was a black seminary in its conception, sponsor a symposium for pastors in which the pastors would come up with a mission statement that would be in agreement across all the denominational lines. Due to multiple priorities and schedules, interference reigned.

We were left with the frustration, knowing it needed to be done and yet we didn't see how to do it. The Lord gave us, what you see as the chapter title at the beginning of this section. It may change a bit, but we are going to try and present this in some way or another and bring it to the attention of the greater church in Baltimore.

**Our Mission**:
**Our mission is to inject the 7 mountains of culture with righteousness and Kingdom principles, such that we cause a Niagara of reversal, repentance and revival that leads to reformation and transformation.**

Just a little bit of explanation. The words "inject" and "Niagara" are used on purpose in this statement, because we want it to spread by its own virtue, if you will;   not by the effort of man, not by the effort of one concerted group, but by the very nature of what it is.   Our mission is to inject the 7 mountains of culture, which is all the culture. This is, by the way, what happened in the reformation, in part, when John Calvin reformed the banking system.   He was primarily responsible for the reformation of the banking system and that's the banking system we have today. That was over 500 years ago. So, it can be done.

What we are saying is, that by moving forward with reversals in all the mountains of culture, we can begin a **Great Reversal** movement, bringing repentance and revival.

**When you put your first love second, you misplace your passion and subject your mission to the whims of conflict!** You should have your mission statement where you can look at and reference it. We talk a great deal about mission, but when you can really lay your hands and <u>your mind</u> on your mission, when conflict occurs, you know how to reject those things not pertaining to your mission. If your circumstances are blockading your mission, something needs to change and it's not your mission.

In our lives we have been blessed to be very versatile people. But we've also been cursed to be very versatile people. Too often our ability to adapt to circumstances and get things done, or to be involved in activities, has gotten in the way of what we should be doing. We've diluted the strength that we had for doing the thing we were called to do, by doing some other good thing. We want to emphasize this, because there are so many slants you can take in this. When we speak of the first love, we're talking about Jesus. The passionate love that we all had when we came to Him, which was so intense that you couldn't shut us up.

When you put that first love **down into second place**, you misplace your passion... "Where did it go?" Then you subject your mission in life to whatever way life's river is flowing-situation ethics. Remember, if you lose your way, Jesus is **The Way**.

## The First and Greatest Commandment

*Thou shall love the Lord, your God, with all your heart, with all your soul (mind), and with all your strength,* (Deuteronomy 6:4)

## The Second Is Like Unto It

*(You shall not take vengeance, nor bear any grudge against the children of your people, but you shall love your neighbor as yourself: I am the Lord.* (Leviticus 19:18)

Let's talk about the first and greatest commandment. You all know what that is, but do you know where it's found in the Old Testament? You see, Jesus was quoting the Old Testament. You shall love the Lord your God, with all your heart, with all your soul, with all your strength. That's in three of the gospels, - Matthew, Mark and Luke. In Matthew 22, Jesus said, *"You shall love the Lord your God, with all your heart, with all your soul and with all your mind".* Now listen, you shall love the Lord your God, that's first, with all of your heart, all of your soul and all of your strength. If you love God, with all your heart, all your soul and all your strength, you are **loving completely**.

> *And the second is like unto it: 'You shall love your neighbor as yourself.* (Matthew 22:40)

The second is like unto it. It doesn't say it's like it, it says it's <u>like unto </u>it.

> *"You shall not take vengeance, nor bear any grudge against the children of your people, but you shall love your neighbor as yourself: I am the LORD."* (Leviticus 19:18)

I am the Lord - I am telling you not to have grudges, and not to take vengeance, but to love your neighbor as yourself, in the way that you love yourself. I don't have a grudge against myself, I certainly am not going to take vengeance on myself; only a crazy person would do that. I care for myself. If I need food or nourishment, I get it. I take care of my needs. He said, "I am the Lord". The same way that you care for Me, care for your neighbor. (New Testament) *"and the second is like unto it, you shall love your neighbor as yourself."* You know that He taught them what He meant when He said, *"your neighbor"*. It included the one nobody wanted to talk to and whom they thought they were better than. Love the Lord your God with all your heart, mind, soul, and strength and proceeding from that, love your neighbor as you love yourself.

**They are written on your HEART and MIND!**

Now what happens to us when we live according to these precepts? On these two commandments hang all the law and the prophets. You see, if you do these two, everything else just falls in line. You don't have to worry yourself with the other commandments, because they will fall in line. I (Robert) love my wife; I love our relationship. I've used this example often. I try my best to do those things that promote our relationship, and I try my best not to do those things that interrupt it. I don't always make it, but I try. When I do mess it up, I go back to her and ask her to forgive me. These laws are written on your heart and your mind. How do you know that they're written on your heart and on your mind? Jeremiah 31:31 says so. It says, that He's going to bring a new covenant and in the New Covenant the law will no longer be written on stones, but will be written right on your heart. That's the New Covenant. So many times, we think because we went to a liturgical church growing up, most of us, that the communion is the new covenant. He says this is blood of the new covenant. (Matt 26:28-29) The new covenant is Jeremiah 31:31, the whole of the law is summed up in love being carried around inside of you, all the time. That's the excitement.

That happened when? On Pentecost. That's why the baptism of the Holy Spirit **cannot be optional**. We, the church, have tried to bring unity to the body of Christ, by dummying down the importance of the Baptism of the Holy Spirit. We cannot reach unity in the Spirit like that. It's not an option, like going to buy a car. You do want all your tires and a real motor but, you can leave off some of the fancier options. When you meet Jesus don't say, well, I'll take the salvation package, but I'm not having the Baptism in the Holy Spirit. Jesus came to give the Holy Spirit to us, so we could live. **He set us free to live with power and He had to empower us to live it.** That came on Pentecost. It's time that we must engage people. Be ready for conflict and blow-back. Someone must speak the truth in love. Ministers are actually taught many classes in evangelical seminaries, line-on-line, how it is wrong to be baptized in the Holy Spirit today. They teach and believe that all Holy Spirit baptism has ceased. Jesus is no longer baptizing with Holy Spirit. That is the meaning of Cessationism. But you know they can't have a complete foundation in the word of God. The scriptures do not say that and it cannot be proven. Some of the deniers call themselves Word People. Somewhere along the way you must challenge them with the truth, but in love. Our God is a supernatural God. Everything He does is supernatural.

### Reversing the first and second commandment

The result is different than what is meant in the scriptures:

- Your relationship to God is bound by human concerns. (Mark 8:33)
- God's law takes second place.
- Your heart and mind are centered on man.

- Love of yourself takes first place.
- Instead of your purpose being God given, it is man skewed!

*But when Jesus turned and looked at his disciples, he rebuked Peter. 'Get behind me, Satan!' he said. '**You do not have in mind the concerns of God,** but <u>merely human concerns.</u>"* (Mark 8:33)NIV

## The result is no longer Christianity!

<u>Good intentions become man centered!</u>

This is the basis of **Humanism, Liberation Theology**, and **Apostasy**.

What follows then is rebellion and witchcraft.

Putting the law of loving man first, becomes the basis of humanism, a false man-centered, pseudo-religion. It becomes the basis for Liberation Theology, putting human concerns before the commandments of God. It morphs into apostasy by placing good deeds at the center. When Jesus turned and looked at His disciples He rebuked Peter, ***"Get behind me Satan, for <u>your mind</u> is not set on <u>God's will</u>, or <u>His values and purposes</u>, but on what pleases man."***(Mark 8:33) Thousands were following Jesus. He was popular with the crowd at that moment. Jesus had just told Peter that He was going to die. "Oh Lord, be it not so!" Peter wanted to change the plan of God. God had that plan before the foundation of the earth, before man was created and sinned, God had the plan on how to save us. Jesus came ready to do God's will and Peter said, "Oh no," to dissuade Jesus. That's what they wanted. That would have pleased them, but it wasn't God's plan. This is what happens when you start trying to do things to please the voice of men.

We've read speculation on why Jesus spoke the name of Satan directly to Peter. We won't go into all the reasons given, but Jesus recognized the demonic influence. This is where a departure was attempted. It was not simply human thought and behavior. Uncorrected, there would be a portal for the enemy to come in and take His mission off course.

## Cessationism encourages <u>humanism</u> in the church. How?

Cessationism encourages humanism in the church. Oh, yes! That's the big thing here. Why do you think people in churches would ever try to support killing babies in their mother's wombs in the light of Jesus' being the Lord of Life? We know He is for life, and yet, a huge amount of the church will stand you down that it's right, because perhaps, someone raped them. There is a lot of rape going on and people being impregnated, but does that give us the right to end life? No! In fact, if we faced up to who the fathers were of all these innocent babies, there'd be a lot of people going to jail. It would be widespread, but after that there would be a chilling fear of God returning once again. It wasn't this way when I, (Annette) grew up in a town of 60,000. If there was a murder, it was on the front page of the paper every day, month, after month. It was a horrific thing. That was the reaction to only one murder. There were not two, three, or six murders a day. No! Why? The culture of the day demanded high moral values. They valued life and they said murder was wrong all the time. We can get back there, "back to the future," but it will take moral outrage and a return to Christian values.

Humanism starts out with the thought that we should do this or that for the betterment of mankind.[15] But as with any devise of man that seeks to avoid God's precepts these attempts go astray and end up creating something far worse than the thing they are trying to correct. When they encounter road blocks or resistance to their intents they resort to some form of brutal enforcement. Expediency gives way to brutality when there is no ultimate authority.[16]

*Expediency gives way to brutality when there is no ultimate authority.*

*When you put your first love second, you misplace your passion and subject your mission to the whims of conflict!*

# CHAPTER 6

# EFFECTS OF REVERSAL

The resistance to believe that God still operates in our situations with supernatural acts, causes the adherents not to experience the God of the impossible! They exchange God working with His people to "being nice" and doing good works. Nice, friendly citizens instead of being world-changers!

Cessationism encourages humanism, following and trying to please men. The resistance to believe that God still operates in our situations with supernatural acts, causes them not to experience the God of the impossible. They exchange God working with His people to being nice and doing good works. Let's face it, it is a very simple choice. You are a human person, with an eternal human spirit and you are going to be led by the Spirit of Jesus Christ or the spirit of the anti-Christ. You can't have it any other way. One or the other; make your choice: nice friendly citizens, or world changers. We were born to change the world, to make a difference!

*The Lord God took the man and put him in the Garden of Eden to work it and take care of it.* (Genesis 2:15)

Who are you and what is your purpose for living? Genesis 1:28, we call that what? The Kingdom Mandate.

It's God giving orders to us, from the very beginning. The principle of first mention, if you will.

> *"Then God blessed them and God said to them, be fruitful, multiply, fill the earth, and subdue it, have dominion over the fish of the sea, over the birds of the air and over every living thing that moves on the earth."* (Genesis 1:28) **We are the custodians of creation!**

### Awaken the seed and open the womb!

It was 2004 here in Maryland, when Chuck Pierce and Dutch Sheets came to our State conducting what was called The 50 State Tour. They traveled to every state in the United States. When they came to Maryland, someone heard this in the spirit and called it out in the meeting. It quickened inside of the leaders who had all of us declare it– **"Awaken the seed, and open the womb, awaken the seed and open the womb, awaken the seed and open the womb!"**

What's the seed? The word of God in you is the seed. Awaken the seed that you are carrying inside of you. When it's awakened, it will grow and it will come to fruition. It will birth out new life; something great will happen. We will be fruitful. Isn't that what the mandate says? That we shall be fruitful! (Gen. 1:28) It is the word that was placed on the map that James Nesbit made for each state. The state of Maryland's word is "Awaken the seed and open the womb." That's the word for Maryland! If you look closely, Maryland surrounds Washington, D.C. which was cut out of Maryland's land; it resembles a womb. Someone, back in 1996, had a vision of Jesus laying on His side down the east coast, and where His womb (if a woman) would be, that was Maryland. Then, 8 years later, came this word by the Spirit to "open the womb".

## Looking in the Spiritual Mirror
(How God Sees You)

, *"now, therefore, if you will indeed obey My voice and keep My covenant, then you shall be a special treasure to Me above all people, for all the earth is Mine, and you shall be to Me a Kingdom of Priests and a holy nation".* (Exodus 19)

You see this is God's original intent for His chosen people. It was not to be one tribe of Priests. It was to be that all of Israel were Priests and a holy nation. You know when Jesus came He reversed the curse. It's written in the New Testament that, we are now a Kingdom of Priests and a holy nation. We are in the Melchizedek order. If you are looking in a spiritual mirror, you see yourself as God sees you.

## You Can Prove God's Will.

*"I beseech you therefore, brethren, by the mercies of God, that ye present your bodies a living sacrifice, holy, acceptable unto God, which is your reasonable service. And be not conformed to this world: but be transformed by the renewing of your mind, that you might prove what is that good, and acceptable, and perfect, will of God".* (Romans 12:1-2)

We need to see ourselves the way God sees us. We need to believe the things He says about us. We can do the things He says we can do. Before this can happen, we need the renewing of our mind. How do you get the renewing of your mind? You get the renewing of your mind by, first of all ingesting God's word, to the point where you know the word; then follow His commands.

## Mission Statement

We stress that every Christian should have a mission statement. If you have been around us any amount of time, you know how much we emphasize knowing your mission in God. We'll help you write it. It's very simple. Use short sentences, understood by a twelve-year old, stating who you are, and why you are here. Our mission statement is: "We prepare people to proclaim and demonstrate the Kingdom of God." Simple. Yes, but it says exactly who we are and what we are about. Anything that comes around us, any opportunity that opens to us that's not part of that mission, we can reject no matter how good it might be, because it's not our calling from God to do that. Our future determines who we are, not our past. God deals with us where He says we are. Our problem is that we focus on our imperfections, don't we? Conflicts and situations do not change our giftings and callings. We already are who He makes us to be. So, Jesus spoke prophetically to Simon Peter a new name that called him forth into his destiny. One definition of Simon, means "blow with the wind". That's who he was before Jesus showed up. Peter got a new name,

"Rock." He wasn't there yet, but God knew what he was to become. He prophesied. Every time He called him "Peter" He was prophesying into his future. Isn't that exciting? I like thinking of Jesus' name. Yeshua, which means salvation. So, every time His mother called Him in from playing, she was calling, "Salvation, Salvation". Yes, she was. Only God can think these things up. , a secure foundation, *"but why do you call me, Lord, Lord, and not do the things which I say? Whoever comes to me, and hears my sayings, and does them, I'll shew you whom he's like: He is like a man building a house, who dug deep, and laid the foundation on the rock"*. Luke 6:46 – 48

## My Future Determines Who I Am, Not My Past

In John, Chapter 8, Jesus tells the woman caught in adultery to go and sin no more. It is **grace** and **love** that produced her new identity, not the law. Since He did not condemn her, she was free to live a new identity. You can make a choice of which way you are going. Are you choosing that poverty and hopelessness will not rule over you?

## Faith v/s Fear - same definition

A poverty mindset is fueled by fear. Faith and fear, it's the same definition. Faith is believing that which hasn't happened will happen. Fear is believing that what hasn't happened will happen; the same thing. It takes as much strength and effort to be afraid as it does to have faith. So, isn't it better to have faith and cast out fear? What to do when fear raises its head?

Bill Johnson says if you have fear, worship. Worship will conquer fear.

## Your ID is very important.

Elijah said,[17] *"How long will you halt between two opinions?"* Your biggest blockade is fear. Worship! You are at your crossroads. We will not be controlled by thoughts of captivity. So, <u>cause your heart to come into freedom</u>. Our hearts must remain free. Must! They can't produce rightly if they are not remaining free. Real war is transforming into your new identity. Your biggest blockade is <u>fear</u>. Come into agreement with what Jesus says about you in His word. *"So **don't be afraid**; you are worth more than many sparrows."* Then in it is written... *"to rescue us from the hand of our enemies, and to enable us to serve him without **fear**.""* (Luke 1:74)

Cast out fear (Matthew 10:31). Fear can be of demonic origin. Command it to leave in Jesus name. If it comes back, call your prayer partners. Where two or more are gathered in His name, there He is right in the midst of you. (Matthew 18:20)

## You are at your crossroads.

*The entrance of Your word gives light. It gives <u>u</u>nderstanding to the simple.* (Psalms 119:130)

God is watching for the choices that we make. There are also divination spirits standing to oppose us at the crossroads. We are at a crossroads now. You sense that, don't you? It's true, everywhere you go

Holy Spirit is speaking that. You have to make a choice. Why doesn't God say, "Okay, go right." He generally doesn't. You have to seek Him. You have to think. In the thinking, in the waiting, in the praying, in the trying to wrestle it out, growth comes forth. The maturity that He's seeking in the mature sons and daughters of the King, comes from having to weigh out things with Him.

> It is the glory of God to conceal a matter, but **the glory of kings is to search out a matter**. (Proverbs 25:2)

In whatever way He leads you to do that – fasting, getting up early, or staying up late, sit before Him. It causes you to grow. When you were a brand-new Christian, He gave you answers, remember? Everything you asked Him, His answers came quickly. But then one day, it didn't quite come that way. You wondered, "What happened, did I sin"? No, God wanted you to grow up and learn how to search out a thing like a king. Sit with the King of Kings and learn His ways as He shares His heart.

*Every Christian should have a mission statement. One simple sentence that includes your gifts and your God sanctified desires.*

# CHAPTER 7

# THE EFFECT OF DISCONNECT AND REVERSAL

## The Political Spirit

Faisel Malick is a former Moslem who has written an excellent book, **The Political Spirit**. The book exposes the supernatural work behind some of our problems. He says this, "Only those who understand the true nature of today's turmoil will be equipped to successfully deal with it." We, as mature sons and daughters of the King, are called to deal with turmoil caused by spiritual influence. What we are not called to do, is to join everyone else in saying, "Oh me, oh my!" We are called to pray, seek God, get together, form think tanks among us, and come up with some solutions that will transform and bring hope to those who are in despair. We will bring lasting solutions, not just temporary ones. It is good to feed the hungry, yes, but they'll be hungry again tomorrow. Someone is called to that, and we thank God for them, as it is so important. But we've got to have some solutions to get some of those people in the breadlines, off the breadlines. Our Father wants lives restored and destinies fulfilled.

We recently proposed to a politician who has the right connections, that a conservative think tank centered on local politics be established. We believe that this individual could raise the funding. Let's pray for that.

We need a think tank for conservative thought and conservative politics. Robert was part of a think tank. He went to a meeting. The participants were actually sitting at a round table and they went around the table telling their names and what they did. By the way, the topic of that conversation was **How to Restart the Economic Engine of Your City**. That's kind of heavy, but that was the topic. Sitting around this table were all very prestigious people, previous judges, a fire chief, president of a bank, county executive, so forth and so on. Each one announced who they were and what their particular insight was. It was very fascinating, and Robert was really thrilling in it and then suddenly, it dawned on him that they were coming in his direction and he didn't have anything to say or so he thought. Fortunately, we had been talking about this very thing. We had come up with a term that is now actually used a lot, it's called the "entitlement mentally". Then it came to Robert's turn to speak. He talked about his experiences in the inner city, and my experiences in the public-school system and how the entitlement mentality affected the lives and thought patterns of the people; how it limited their vision. As he spoke this, a "hush" fell over this exalted group of people and everybody was remarking, "Amazing, we see it". It was quite fascinating. You don't have to have a title, or think that you are really prepared, but God in you, who knows the answer and has all the solutions, is ready to speak a word out of your mouth that can actually ignite all the others.

There are others who are fully equipped to add to the idea you bring. Others have the wherewithal to empower that and bring it forth. It is exciting to think about.

## Your Mission – His Mission

Remember, that we're talking about a reversal of God's given command, and the effect of that reversal. His mission in us is to reverse the reversal. We have the responsibility to put it back the way it was intended to be. Your mission is His mission. The more aligned you become with God's word, the more attuned you will be to the leading of His Spirit. You will then have more clarity about how you can accomplish His will concerning your life.

## The Nature of the Warfare

The nature of warfare is the releasing of the true government of God; not just the releasing of it, but establishing it. Put down the roots that can go on and on. As it says in Isa. 9, *"that of His government and peace there will be no end"*. It just keeps developing and setting down more roots. The place where God's will and tender mercies can once more flow without interference from the enemy.[18] Think of that!

Opposing God's government is what Faisal Malick calls, "The great handshake." We're talking about spirits and how they work. The great handshake that affects us is the **political spirit** and the **religious spirit** coming together! When we're talking about the political spirit, we're not talking about politics, or political parties or platforms. We're talking about an operational spirit. If you want to know more about it, read Faisal Malick. His book tells us very clearly that this spirit gained its power in the reign of Herod.

He talks a lot about Herod and why that spirit developed and gained power. Incidentally, for those who don't know, when it speaks of Herod in the bible in the New Testament, actually throughout the New Testament, there are six different men called Herod, they are not all one person; they are all related. The Herods just seem to get worse as the story unfolds. The political spirit was working through each Herod mightily and the Political Spirit also worked with the Pharisees, the religious party. It also happens when churches get mixed up in politics. I'm not talking about taking a righteous stand for a righteous cause. That is correct. When churches become immersed in the platforms of political parties and political personalities, and then become promotional of one party over another, this is not only disruptive, it is counter directional to what God has called us to be and do. You know both parties that we have, both the Democratic and Republican parties, should be righteous parties. We need to talk about righteousness and justice. They are the foundation of God's throne. (Ps.89:14)

There are things that get put into a party platform, their foundation, and which they change with the election cycle. When there is a presidential election, they put new things in, and can take old things out. I think that in the past, the average party platform was about two-pages long. Do you know how many pages are in the current Democratic Party platform? Fifty-one! So, you know almost no one is going to read that. The Republican Party's platform is also too long. Something concise that the people can remember is needed; a return to simplicity.

## The Political and Religious Spirit

Let's look at what these do and what they are. The political spirit is an invisible mastermind that wants to kill whatever God is doing at all costs. It uses many spirits to help accomplish this. The political spirit will usually form a coalition of spirits. A stronghold. It's a stronghold, a major stronghold operating behind that with which you're dealing. It's not just one thing to be cast out. One attribute of the political spirit is that it always creates alliances. Those with this spirit are concerned with what people think about them and are occupied with reputation and public opinion. The reason behind this is that it wants to get everyone's power. A political spirit will employ other spirits to accomplish this purpose. A political spirit will use Jezebel. It wants to shut up the mouth of the prophets and kill all the prophetic words and all the prophetic revelation on which we can move forward. Political spirits will use political beliefs and pride to split a congregation or a multi-church alliance. The political spirit will hide its real intent behind the intent and actions of others. The political spirit always has a hidden agenda that you will not be able to discern with your natural senses. That's why you've got to be sharp in the Holy Spirit.

The religious spirit often says we must do this or that to please God. It picks out an obscure passage and misapplies it to a situation. The religious spirit seeks the ritualistic approach and criticizes in private conversation. A religious spirit, for example, will make a person grow overly pious and religious. Then, in a gradual step-by-step process, the person will go from being a true believer to a tool in the hand of the devil, distorting the truth to the point of destroying lives. This is what happens with cults. The religious spirit is controlling and it makes the people puppets. When an objective is achieved, the political spirit will turn on the religious spirit. So, they aren't really in unity. The political spirit uses the religious spirits of the people in the religious pious community, until it has its way and gains power! Then it will turn against all religion because it wants everything for itself. When that happens you are going to be in the midst of a battle-royal.

## Reverse complacency with passionate love!

The political spirit will challenge biblical principles in favor of humanistic reasoning, such as marriage vows. One of the biggest things that is happening among our younger people, people age 30 and down, is that trial marriages are a good thing. We'll try it out to see how it works. They don't take any vows. They make no commitment. On several occasions, we have married people who have lived together. Every one of those situations, where we did that, the marriages only lasted a year or two. Beware the strategy of Balaam. The strategy of Balaam was sexual immorality and food sacrificed to idols. That is how Balaam suggested that Balak attack the Jewish people, the Israelites, because it was the breaking of covenant. When covenant was broken, God's protection was no longer on the Israelites.

Let me tell you just a little bit about Balaam. You've all read the story of Balaam. He was a world-famous prophet. He lived over 400 miles away from Balak's territory. That's a 21-day journey, one way in that time. He was well known for his effectiveness as a prophet. He was not a false prophet, he was a real prophet. He was a bad one, but he was a real one. He loved money. The worst thing about it was that his gift was for sale. In Revelation 3, it says, one of the ways the church will lose its lampstand is by following the precepts of Balaam. Remember this too, it took an ignorant ass to correct him, no matter how accurate a prophet he was. It's a great story and I suggest you re-read it. There's over three full chapters about Balaam and at least six other mentions throughout scripture. Balaam is not a minor figure. He's a very major figure in scripture. Balaam was a real prophet, not a false one. Not only could he hear from God but he did what God told him. The problem with Balaam was <u>that his gift was for sale.</u> He told Balak how to get Israel to break their covenant. (Rev. 2:14, Num.31:16, 2Peter 2:15) When that happens, demonic activity is the direct result. When you break covenant, or you allow covenant to be broken, the result is demonic activity. Expect it.

**Reverse the reversal.**

All sin has corporate consequences. - all sin! It's a lie in the church that there are private sins behind closed doors that don't matter to anyone but the people doing them. **That's a lie. All sin has corporate consequences.** If there is sin in the church, portals are open for demonic influence. Demons gain access through portals opened by iniquitous actions.

Reverse the atmosphere of your city, town and state. Prophesy to it!

Make it a joyful place to live. *Rebuild your cities![19]*

*Woe to those complacent in Zion.[20]*
What is complacency? It's not passion is it? It's the opposite of passion. You can reverse complacency with passionate love. What can cause us to be complacent? Isa. 14:17 implies Satan made the world like a wilderness and overthrew its cities. Would you believe that could be Baltimore, Washington, D.C., or other major cities? We can reverse the atmosphere of cities, towns and states. Prophesy to it, don't say, "This is a city of murder and violence"! Who can't look and see then say? Anybody! It takes faith that breaks the bonds of wickedness to reverse the way it looks, by you prophesying to it. Make it a joyful place to live and rebuild your cities, as it says in Isa.

58. We can do that. The broken-down places can be rebuilt and it begins with you today.

*Defend the poor and the needy. "Is not that what it means to <u>know me</u>? (Jer. 22:16)*

Our primary mission is to <u>know God</u>.

"*Defend the poor and the needy. Is not that what it means <u>to know me</u>?"* Knowing. Jesus says, "Isn't this what it means to know me, God". Defend the poor and the needy. In the cities is where we see violence and murder as a result of innocent blood shed on the land. Remember that righteousness and justice are the foundation of His throne. Our primary mission is to know God. That's why we're here – to know God. So, when you think about righteousness and justice being the foundation of His throne[21], your mind usually just turns to heaven. You think of the throne room, and the basis for His sitting there – His righteousness and justice. He's carved this in our hearts through the baptism of the Holy Spirit.

We have a friend, Dr. Chuck Thurston, MD., who has written a wonderful book which he also made into a video. It is called "Body Codes". As a doctor, he assures us that, we have a throne in our human bodies that is our physical heart which is surrounded by a crown. This crown is made up of coronary arteries which literally means crown. This signifies a throne in the middle of your chest. "Come sit on the throne of my heart, Jesus". Who can think these things up? God. We're discovering now what

He's known all along. That aside, righteousness and justice are in your heart when He's on the throne.

We can have the things to do that are going to help the poor and the needy. The church is the joy that was set before Jesus. The church was included in God's eternal plan in the eons of past time before the world was created. If ministers in the church would catch the heart throb of Jesus, their efforts would not be in promoting their doctrines, their denominations, their revelations or experiences. But it would be in building up and unifying the church. I wish I had thought that up, but that was     Apostle Bill Hamon in his book, The Eternal Church.

Put God first. Demonstrate that with prayer and worship. Teach the bible in depth.    Teach intercession and spiritual warfare.    Build relationships. You know that's all about apostleship. Can you tell that is what our Alliance is about? Building relationships. We expect that when we bring you together, you are going to talk to each other. We ask you to really get something going.    Invite someone over to your house, to your church, to your home group. Invite one another to minister. Get to know each other, not just as ministers of the gospel, but as people with whom Jesus would hang out. Jesus didn't like the religious stuff, He liked good. He said only God was good, didn't He?    So, build relationships.

**Awaken the seed and open the womb!**

*PRAYER:*

*Lord, we pray that You would circumcise our hearts afresh and give us hearts of flesh that can respond to Your cry and cut away the stony hearts that are in us. Lord, that we might be like the people that wept and mourned over the condition of Zion when Ezekiel saw the angel come to anoint the head of all those who mourned in Zion. They mourned over the condition that made God mournful. You said that only those who were anointed with oil would not be destroyed. So, Lord, we sit and see the condition of the church and the condition of the cities and we turn away. Or we give a little prayer and then we don't think about it for another year. Today, we seek Your heart. We want Your heart. We want a heart of flesh that matches our Father's heart and we come to You to get it, Lord. We ask You to awaken the sound of the morning Shofar inside of our hearts, inside of our spirits. We say, "Pull us into alignment with You, O God. Pull us into alignment". We would be of one heart, one mind, and one breath. We want to be of one breath with Holy Spirit, so that people will know that you have sent us to them. Thank you, Jesus! Amen.*

# Demons gain access through portals opened by iniquitous actions.

# PART 3

# RESTORATION!

## REVERSING CRISIS THROUGH COVENANT RESTORATION

How do we restore ourselves to these original intents of the Father?

# CHAPTER 8

# GOD'S ORIGINAL INTENT

## Custodians of Creation

*26 Then God said, "Let Us make man in Our image, according to Our likeness; let them have dominion over the fish of the sea, over the birds of the air, and over the cattle, over [g]all the earth and over every creeping thing that creeps on the earth." 27 So God created man in His own image; in the image of God He created him; male and female He created them. 28 Then God blessed them, and God said to them, "Be fruitful and multiply; fill the earth and subdue it; have dominion over the fish of the sea, over the birds of the air, and over every living thing that [h]moves on the earth."* (Genesis 1:26-28)

God told man to:

1.  Be fruitful.
2.  Multiply.
3.  Fill the earth.
4.  Subdue it.
5.  Have dominion.

In other words, take care of it, and utilize it. This is what is referred to as the Dominion Mandate. In effect, God made us custodians of His creation. It is our mandate to take care of the earth and all that is within it but to also utilize it and cause it to bear fruit.

Jesus told His followers, in the parable of the Talents (Mina), to "*Occupy til I come.*" This means to utilize or put it to use. Remember that the faithful (full of faith) servants that did wisely were rewarded with authority. God designed us to wisely manage His creation.

### Kingdom of Priests

> *5 Now therefore, if you will indeed obey My voice and keep My covenant, then you shall be a special treasure to Me above all people; for all the earth is Mine. 6 And you shall be to Me a Kingdom of priests and a holy nation.' These are the words which you shall speak to the children of Israel."* (Exodus 19:5-6)

### God's chosen were to be a Kingdom of Priests. Not just one tribe but all of them.

> *19 This hope we have as an anchor of the soul, both sure and steadfast, and which enters the Presence behind the veil, 20 where the forerunner has entered for us, even Jesus, having become High Priest forever according to the order of Melchizedek.* (Hebrews 6:19-20)

*15 And it is yet far more evident if, in the likeness of Melchizedek, there arises another priest 16 who has come, not according to the law of a fleshly commandment, but according to the power of an endless life. 17 For He testifies: "You are a priest forever according to the order of Melchizedek."* (Hebrews 7:15-17)


*"Behold, the days are coming, says the LORD, when I will make a new covenant with the house of Israel and with the house of Judah— 9 not according to the covenant that I made with their fathers in the day when I took them by the hand to lead them out of the land of Egypt; because they did not continue in this My covenant, and I disregarded them, says the LORD. 10 For is the covenant that I will make with the house of Israel after those days, says the LORD: I will put <u>My laws in their mind and write them on their hearts;</u> and I will be their God, and they shall be My people.*

*11 Therefore, if perfection were through the Levitical priesthood (for under it the people received the law), what further need was there that another priest should rise according to the order of Melchizedek, and not be called according to the order of Aaron? 12 For <u>**the priesthood being changed, of necessity**</u> there is also a change of the law. 13 For He of whom these things are spoken belongs to another tribe, from which no man has [o]officiated at the altar.* (Hebrews 6:11-13)


*"...To Him who loved us and washed us from our sins in His own blood, 6 and has made us <u>kings and priests</u> to His God and Father, to Him be glory and dominion forever and ever. Amen."* (Revelation 1:5)

*"And have made us kings and priests to our God;
And we shall reign on the earth."* (Revelation 5:10)

His original intent was for His chosen to be a Kingdom of priests. Through Jesus, our new High Priest, we are restored to be priests of a New Covenant. We are priests of the Order of Melchizedek, not of the Order of Levi. This new order of priests does not function (or worship out of obligation) as the previous order, but rather worships as an expression of relationship with the Father.[22]

## Restore

How do we restore ourselves to these intents of the Father? The simple answer is that we can't, at least not without Jesus. You see, Jesus death on the cross and the shedding of innocent blood as an atonement for the lost condition of the human race, is the only path for restoration. But that's not all there is. <u>There must be a new nature to replace the old</u>.

1. Put aside traditions of men.
2. Release covenant and restore creation.
3. Bring order into chaos and crisis.

## Covenant: A Unilateral Relationship

1. Garden Covenant  –  Custodians of Creation

2. Noahic Covenant  –  The Rainbow

3. Abrahamic Covenant  –  Descendants numerous           as stars or grains of sand

4. Mosaic Covenant  -  The Law

5. Davidic Covenant  -  Descendants on the throne

6. New Covenant  -  Written on your heart and minds

## Garden Covenant

1. Be fruitful, multiply, subdue, have dominion and replenish.
2. "I have given every green herb for food."
3. Don't eat from the tree of the knowledge of good     and evil.

## The Noahic Covenant

It is unique in applying to all humanity, while the other covenants are principally promises by God to His chosen.

*I will sing of the mercies of the Lord forever; With my mouth will I make known Your faithfulness to all generations. [2] For I have said, "Mercy shall be built up forever; Your faithfulness You shall establish in the very heavens." [3] "I have made a covenant with My chosen, I have sworn to My Servant David:*
*(Psalm 89)*

## Abrahamic Covenant

In Genesis 15 God covenants with Abram (before his name was changed):

*"... one who will come from your own body shall be your heir."* **5** *Then He brought him outside and said, "Look now toward heaven, and count the stars if you are able to number them." And He said to him, "So shall your descendants be."* **6** *And he believed in the LORD, and He accounted it to him for righteousness.*

## GOD TO DAVID

*I have found My servant David; With My holy oil I have anointed him,* **21** *With whom My hand shall be established; Also My arm shall strengthen him.* **22** *The enemy shall not outwit him, Nor the son of wickedness afflict him.* **23** *I will beat down his foes before his face, And plague those who hate him.* **24** *"But My faithfulness and My mercy shall be with him, And in My name his horn shall be exalted.* **25** *Also I will set his hand over the sea, And his right hand over the rivers.* **26** *He shall cry to Me, 'You are my Father, My God, and the rock of my salvation.'* **27** *Also I will make him My firstborn, The highest of the kings of the earth.* **28** *My mercy I will keep for him forever, And My covenant shall stand firm with him.* **29** *His seed also I will make to endure forever, And his throne as the days of heaven.* **30** *"If his sons forsake My law And do not walk in My judgments,* **31** *If they break My statutes And do not keep My commandments,* **32** *Then I will punish their transgression with the rod, And their iniquity with stripes.* **33** *Nevertheless My lovingkindness I will not utterly take from him, nor allow My faithfulness to fail.* **34** *My covenant I will not* *break, nor alter the word that has gone out of My lips. Once I have sworn by My holiness; I will not lie to David:* [36] *His seed shall endure forever, And his throne as the sun before Me;* [37] *It shall be established forever like the moon, Even like the faithful witness in the sky." Selah*! (Psalm 89:20-37)

## Christian View of the New Covenant

*"For this is the covenant that I will make with the house of Israel after those days, says the LORD: I will put My laws in their mind and write them on their hearts; and I will be their God, and they shall be My people."* (Hebrews 8:10) *(Also see Jeremiah 31:31)*

## A new relationship between God and mankind:

1. Mediated by Jesus
2. Includes all people, both Jews and Gentiles (as grafted in)
3. A sincere declaration that one believes in Jesus Christ as Lord and God

## The Mediator's Death Necessary

*For where there is a testament, there must also of necessity be the death of the testator.* [17] *For a testament is in force after men are dead, since it has no power at all while the testator lives.* [18] *Therefore not even the first covenant was dedicated without blood.* (Hebrews 9:16)

*And according to the law almost all things are purified with blood, and without shedding of blood there is no remission.* (Hebrews 9:22)

## Why Crime and Violence?

Iniquity begets violence. Iniquity opens a portal of entrance for the enemy. The result is demonic infestation. This causes a vacuum of benefit from God's promise. Order is lost and chaos will reign.

In accordance with the active law of redemption, God promises (covenants) that He will redeem the land (restore order) when His people turn from their wicked ways (2 Chronicles 7:14).

In order to bring city-wide restoration, it would take a corporate act of a significant body of believers. First, we *uncover* how the enemy took it. Then corporately *repent* for it. Followed by a *commitment to sustain* the redeemed territory. In order to reverse it and take it back, a plan of maintenance is necessary or <u>the enemy can return</u>!

If a covenant is entered into without complete dedication, then the benefits of the covenant are null and withheld. Covenant may have stipulations, but not necessarily, mutual benefit.

The covenant maker provides benefit to the receiver without regard to benefit for himself. He may benefit from the full participation of the other.

Contracts and covenants are not the same things. Here are some fundamental differences:[23]

- While a contract is legally binding, a covenant is a spiritual agreement.
- A contract is an agreement between parties while a covenant is a pledge.
- A contract is an agreement you can break, while a covenant is a perpetual promise.
- You seal a covenant, while you sign a contract.
- A contract is a mutually beneficial relationship, while a covenant is something you fulfill.
- A contract exchanges one good for another, while a covenant is giving oneself to the other.
- You can opt out of a contract, while a covenant is about having the strengths to hold up your part of the promise.
- One can stop paying in a contract when one party is not fulling their part in a deal. However, in a covenant, the party not getting their needs met, supports the failing party so that they can meet their obligations.

## God Is Always Faithful!

Though man is by nature a covenant breaker, God demonstrates His mercy and grace by fulfilling the terms of the human side of the covenant. All that God has done in saving us through grace, since the revelation of the Abrahamic covenant, is the result and product of it…everything that God has done since to the present moment, He has done in order to fulfill His covenant to Abraham (and thus His eternal plan of redemption).

Taken together, the covenants are a progressive unity. The principles upon which God governs His relationship with man are the same from covenant to covenant.

The terms of the covenants are so important to God that He took it upon Himself to fulfill all of the terms of the covenants, including the curses.

When we enter into the covenant, we enter through Messiah Jesus. In Him, we find the fulfillment of God's promises. It is He whom we must imitate in covenant faithfulness.

*Taken together, the covenants are a progressive unity. The principles upon which God governs His relationship with man are the same from covenant to covenant.*

# CHAPTER 9

# LOVING GOD FIRST

## The First and Greatest Commandment

*You shall love the Lord your God with all your heart, mind, soul, and strength.* (Deuteronomy 6:5)

*You shall **love** the Lord your **God** with all your heart, with all your soul, and with all your strength.* (Matthew 22:3, Mark 12:30, Luke 10:27)

## The Second is like unto it

*You shall not take vengeance, nor bear any grudge against the children of your people, but <u>you shall love your neighbor as yourself</u>:  I am the Lord.* (Leviticus 19:18)

*And the second is like   unto   it:  'You   shall love your neighbor as yourself.'* (Matthew 22:39, Mark 12:31, Luke 10:27)

*On these two commandments <u>hang all the Law and the Prophets</u>.* (Matthew 22:40)
•

        *And*

*They are written on your <u>heart</u> and <u>mind</u>!* (Jeremiah 31:31)

## Reversal of the First and Second Commandment

The result is:

1. Your relationship to God is bound by <u>human concerns</u>.
2. God's law takes <u>second</u> place.
3. Your heart and mind are centered on man.
4. Love of yourself takes first place.
5. Instead of your purpose being God given, it is man skewed!

   <u>The result is no longer Christianity</u>!

Good intentions become man centered and are the basis of:

- Humanism
- Liberation Theology
- Apostasy

A rejection of absolute authority leads to anarchy and chaos.

## Cessationism encourages <u>humanism</u> in the church. How?

The resistance to believe that God still operates in our situations with supernatural acts, causes one not to experience the God of the impossible! They exchange God's covenant with His people to "being nice" and doing good works.

When someone begins to reason based on postmodern thinking, the progressive rejecting of authority and any basis of morality, begins. <u>This is a threshold to anarchy</u>.

> *What starts as a nibbling at the forbidden snack, becomes a feasting on the fruit of the tree of the knowledge of good and evil.* [24]

In answer to the adversary's eternal question, **"Did God really say...?"**

The resounding reply must always be,

**"Yes, He did!"**

Conflicts and situations do <u>not</u> change my gifts and callings.

## How to pray effectively

In situations where Jesus has given the believer specific authority (such as healing and deliverance), speak directly to the situation with boldness. Do not ask Jesus or the Father to do it, when He has told <u>you</u> to do it.

> *And these signs will follow those who [a]believe: In My name they will cast out demons; they will speak with new tongues;* [18] *they[b] will take up serpents; and if they drink anything deadly, it will by no means hurt them; they will lay hands on the sick, and they will recover.* (Mark 16:17)

Make declarations in accordance and agreement with scriptural principles.

Read Robert Henderson's book, <u>Accessing the Courts of Heaven</u> and similar books. Become comfortable with this type of intercession. <u>Remember</u>: The court's verdict will be the result of only what has been presented.

## Your Mission – His Mission

If you are the rules and regulations person, you are not going to see the fullness of the Kingdom of God, nor experience the real spirit of His company.

## Put God First!

- Demonstrate prayer and worship.
- Teach the bible in depth.
- Teach intercession and spiritual warfare.
- Build relationships.

## The Kingdom

It is written within you, and waiting for you to **unlock and release it!**

> *And He said, "To **you** it has been **given** to know **the** mysteries of **the Kingdom** of God, but to **the** rest it is **given** in parables, that 'Seeing **they** may not see, and hearing **they** may not understand.'* (Luke 8:10)

> *"Do not fear, little flock, for it is **your** Father's good pleasure to **give you the Kingdom**.*" (Luke 12:32)

> *But without faith it **is** impossible to please Him, for **he** who comes to God **must believe that He is**, and **that He is** a rewarder of those who diligently seek Him.* (Hebrews 11:6)

**How can God give us the Kingdom if it is locked up in parables?**

The answer is in the scriptures and the way that God reveals Himself to mankind. God is a covenant God who presents His covenant to man, so that man can live in the promised blessings. Thus the Kingdom is given where the King (God) is enthroned and rules.

What do you think is the central theme of the Scriptures? The scriptures begin with creation. The activity of creation culminates with the creation of man. The introductory scripture ends with man finding his place in a perpetual heavenly environment. Throughout the scriptural narrative, God relates to man in a covenantal manner giving man the opportunity to partake in God's blessing. God even provides a means to return when man strays away from the path of righteousness. While God does not pull the strings as a heavenly puppeteer, He does clearly reveal His will and displeasure.

*The central theme of scripture is the relationship between God and man.*

### God's Original Intent

1.  Man was (and is) created for fellowship with God.
2.  Man was (and is) the custodian of creation.
3.  God's chosen were (and are) to be a Kingdom of priests.

God is a covenant God. He is always true to His covenant promises. God makes these covenants (promises) to establish and ensure His relationship with man. He made us, therefore, He knows what's best for us. He says clearly that he has a plan for us, a plan for a hope and a future![25]

*A man of God must walk in the plan of God, to see the Kingdom of God!*

# CHAPTER 10

## GOD ESTABLISHES BOUNDARIES

### The Boundaries of Our Relationship

The commandments of God establish the boundaries of our relationship. Within the relationship boundaries, we are assured of His faithfulness to keep His covenant. Without the boundaries, we can also be assured that the curse will be present. So, within the boundaries is peace, but without is curse resulting in chaos.

How do you present the Gospel of the Kingdom to someone who has never heard it before? Present the Gospel as Jesus originally intended with Love, Miracles, Signs, and Wonders! The Kingdom of God is **righteousness, peace,** and **joy.**

### ♪ Righteousness, Peace & Joy ♪
Official lyrics by Ron Kenoly[26]

> Righteousness, peace, joy
> In the Holy Ghost
> Righteousness, peace and joy
> In the Holy Ghost
> That's the Kingdom of God
>
> Don't you want to be a part
> Of the Kingdom
> Don't you want to be a part

Of the Kingdom
Don't you want to be a part
Of the Kingdom
Come on everybody

There's love in the Kingdom
So much love in the Kingdom
There's love in the Kingdom
Come on everybody
There's peace in the Kingdom
So much peace in the Kingdom
There's peace in the Kingdom
Come on everybody
There's joy in the Kingdom
So much joy in the Kingdom
There's joy in the Kingdom
Come on everybody

There's love in God's Kingdom
So much love (2)
Come on everybody
There's peace in God's Kingdom
So much peace (2)
Come on everybody
There's joy in God's Kingdom
So much joy (2)
Come on everybody

I'm an heir of the Kingdom
So glad I'm an heir
Of the Kingdom

I'm an heir of the Kingdom
Come on everybody

Righteousness peace and joy in the Holy Ghost that is the Kingdom of God.

## Boundaries

When a righteous sovereign establishes a Kingdom, he sets its boundaries. He secures those borders from attack by the enemy. Then he establishes the rule of law to conduct his Kingdom business and for the conduct of his citizens. Inside the boundaries of the Kingdom are righteousness, peace, and joy. Outside are lawlessness, falsehood, chaos, and sadness.

While Jesus told us a lot about what His Kingdom is like (through His parables), He never said exactly what the Kingdom was. It was St. Paul who described the Kingdom in Romans chapter 14.

> ... *for the Kingdom of God is not eating and drinking, but righteousness and peace and joy in the Holy Spirit.* (Romans 14: 17)

**Let's examine those three elements of the Kingdom.**

God is righteous and demonstrates righteousness through His covenant promises to which He is always faithful. Abraham was accounted righteous because of his faith in God that God would fulfill His covenant. [27]

## Righteousness
And the Scripture was fulfilled which says, *"Abraham believed God, and it was accounted to him for righteousness."* (James 2:23)

And he was called the friend of God.

1. God cannot fail to fulfill His covenant promises.
2. You can depend on it.
3. When we stay within the covenant boundaries, we are eligible to participate in the covenant blessings.
4. The Law (now written on our hearts) establishes the boundaries of the (Kingdom) covenant.
5. God gives us His word and the prophetic to affirm and demonstrate His love for us.
6. The prophetic demonstrates and accelerates His relationship toward us.[28]
7. God gives us the power to get wealth in order to establish His covenant.

*"And you shall remember the Lord your God, for it is He who gives you power to get wealth that **He may establish His covenant** which He swore to your fathers, as it is this day.* (Deuteronomy 8:18)

## Peace

The Peace of the Kingdom is God's *shalom*. It is peaceful because the outcome is certain.

1. Shalom- Nothing missing, nothing broken, nothing out of order
2. Shalom – destroys the source of chaos.
3. Within the boundaries is shalom.
4. Outside the boundaries is chaos.

## Joy in the Holy Spirit

1. Holy Spirit brings gifts and empowers the believer.
2. Within the boundaries is power and security.
3. Outside the boundaries is weakness and vulnerability.
4. There is joy in strength and security.

The Kingdom is described in Revelation 22:14

*14 Blessed are those who [g]do His commandments, that they may have the right to the tree of life, and may enter through the gates into the city. 15 [h]* <u>*But outside*</u> *are dogs and sorcerers and sexually immoral and murderers and idolaters, and whoever loves and practices a lie.*

### Kingdom Parables

*Now when He was asked by the Pharisees when the Kingdom of God would come, He answered them and said, "The Kingdom of God does not come with observation;* [21] *nor will they say,* [a]*'See here!' or 'See there!' For indeed, the Kingdom of God is* [b]*within you."* (Luke 17: 20)

The law is written on our hearts. It is our responsibility to establish the Kingdom that Jesus described which was very likely different than the Kingdom His followers expected Him to establish and rule. He told them that the Kingdom was within them. It is evident that the appearance of the Kingdom is constantly changing as new believers are added to its ranks. The appearance may change but the principles are eternal.

The Kingdom of God is like a great ball of sticky tape, rolled up tightly, sticky side out, rolling down a hillside, gathering to itself everything in its path. It looks very different at the bottom of the hill than it did at the top.

The Kingdom of God is ever changing, ever increasing. God once told me, "If you are propping up an old structure, get out from under it, before it collapses upon you." He was talking about the church and the paradigms of our Kingdom concepts. He wants us to get a new perspective on what He meant when He said *"On this rock I will build my ecclesia."* The foundational rock was the revelation of the identity of Jesus that Peter had received from the Father. He is the Messiah, the "promised one." Jesus' mission, which involved His death on the cross, was to establish a pathway for God's Kingdom to emerge from within the believer. For this to happen, we needed the power of God to transform our minds (Romans 12:2). He told the disciples, after He had prayed for them and before His Ascension, "Go and wait for the power." They did not know what "the power" would be or what it would look like. But they went and waited expectantly for ten days.[29]

The earthly mission of Jesus was threefold.

- First, through His earthly teaching, He set up the precedents for Kingdom understanding.
- Secondly, His suffering and death, fulfilled the old covenant conditions of man's return to covenantal standing by taking all the curses upon Himself.
- Thirdly, He ushered in the **abiding presence of God through the Baptism of the Holy Spirit**. This is the gateway for the establishment of the new and better covenant promised in Jeremiah 31.

**The Kingdom of God is like a boxing ring.**

A boxing ring is surrounded by ropes, which are the boundaries of the ring. Within the ring, the conduct of the participants is regulated by very strict rules and guarded over by a referee. Outside the ropes, there are no rules: it is every man for himself (chaos rules). The boxer who is constantly on the ropes (testing the boundaries) is unlikely to win the match. While the one who takes command of the center of the ring is much more likely to be the winner. Within the ring there is order.

Life is like that. When we are constantly on the boundaries of the Kingdom, trying to live as close to the <u>worldly borders as possible,</u> or outside of it, then chaos is ever our partner. Peace and righteousness accompany us when we are <u>in the center of God's intent,</u> intentionally living with God, His way.

I like to explain it this way: I love my wife and I value our relationship. I don't do the things that damage that relationship (at least, that's my intent). When I do err, I confess my error and ask her forgiveness and she is willing and quick to do so. I do those things which enhance our relationship. I do not need a written set of rules for this because I know intuitively, and from experience, what is right and what is not.

So, God establishes the boundaries of our relationship with Him through the commandments and covenants. When we operate within those boundaries, we are in His Kingdom presence. Within is righteousness, peace and joy. Without is duplicity, chaos and sorrow.

*The abiding presence of God through the Baptism of the Holy Spirit, is the gateway for the establishment of the new and better covenant promised in Jeremiah 31.*

*And we know that all things work together for good to those who love God, to those who are the called according to His purpose.*

(Romans 8:28)

# CHAPTER 11

## THE KINGDOM OF GOD IS LIKE...

### Kingdom Traits

Although it is not often interpreted this way, Jesus' Sermon on the Mount was a Kingdom description. Apostle Tommy Reid, in his book, *Radical Revolution,*[30] makes the point that Jesus was describing aspects of Kingdom citizens in the Beatitudes. These were radical concepts for His followers to assimilate.

The Kingdom of God is like:
A rebellious son
A sower
A mustard seed
A landowner
A fresh baked loaf of bread

### Two Sons

*28 "But what do you think? A man had two sons, and he came to the first and said, 'Son, go, work today in my vineyard.' 29 He answered and said, 'I will not,' but afterward he regretted it and went. 30 Then he came to the second and said likewise. And he answered and said, 'I go, sir,' but he did not go. 31 Which of the two did the will of his father?" They said to Him, "The first." Jesus said to them, "Assuredly, I say to you that tax collectors and harlots enter the Kingdom of God before you. 32 For John came to you in the way of righteousness, and you did not believe him; but tax collectors and*

*harlots believed him; and <u>when you saw it</u>, <u>you did</u>
<u>not</u> afterward <u>relent and believe him</u>.*
(Matthew 21:28-32)

## Our Response

We interpret this to mean that the whole world is our winepress, and Father is calling us to work in it. Are we ready to work? Or are we reluctant to go? Do we have good intentions but don't follow through? It's not enough to sit in church on Sunday morning! It's not enough to get blessed in the service.

We can miss the call.

## A Certain Sower-

The Parable of the Sower

*And when a great multitude had gathered, and they had come to Him from every city, He spoke by a parable: 5 "A sower went out to sow his seed. And as he sowed, some fell by the wayside; and it was trampled down, and the birds of the air devoured it. 6 Some fell on rock; and as soon as it sprang up, it withered away because it lacked moisture 7 And some fell among thorns, and the thorns sprang up with it and choked it. 8 But others fell on good ground, sprang up, and yielded a crop a hundredfold." When He had said these things He cried, "He who has ears to hear, let him hear!"* (Matthew 13:4-8)

The Purpose of Parables

*9 Then His disciples asked Him, saying, "What does this parable mean?" 10 And He said, "To you it has been given to know the mysteries of the Kingdom of God, but to the rest it is given in parables, that 'Seeing they may not see, and hearing they may not understand."* (Matthew 13:9-10)

The Parable of the Sower Explained

*11 "Now the parable is this: The seed is the word of God. 12     Those by the wayside are the ones who hear; then the devil comes and takes away the word out of their hearts, lest they should believe and be saved.*

*13 But the ones on the rock are those who, when they hear, receive the word with joy; and these have no root, who believe for a while and in time of temptation fall away.*

*14 Now the ones that fell among thorns are those who, when they have heard, go out and are choked with cares, riches, and pleasures of life, and bring no fruit to maturity.*

*15 But the ones that fell on the good ground are those who, having heard the word with a noble and good heart, keep it and bear fruit with patience* (Matthew 13:11-15)

## Mustard Seed

*Another parable He put forth to them, saying: "The Kingdom of heaven is like a mustard seed, which a man took and sowed in his field, 32 which indeed is the least of all the seeds; but when it is grown it is greater than the herbs and becomes a tree, so that the birds of the air come and nest in its branches."* (Matthew 13:31-32)

Four Elements - a seed, a field, a tree, birds.

First, there was the seed. Inside the seed was the fullness of a predestined outcome. Every seed has a potential and a destiny. When the seed is planted in good soil, and given the light and the rain in due season, it will develop a root system; the root system will grow downward and outward to support a great plant even to the size of a tree.

Second, the field owner is the Father, and the field is His domain. He has already made the field ready for planting by plowing it up. He knows that by preparing the soil, He can expect to gain the maximum expectation of the seed to produce a tree which will produce more seed and return a crop that can provide abundant return on His investment. Will His investment in us bear fruit?

Thirdly, the very existence of the tree goes beyond the crop and provides shelter and protection. God's word is like that. Not only does The Word bring a new crop into the Kingdom, it gives shelter through instruction and effects the lives it touches.

Fourthly, the birds represent people, the souls of whom are sheltered and gathered together in a mutually beneficial society.

### The Parable of the Workers in the Vineyard
*"For the Kingdom of heaven is like a landowner who went out early in the morning to hire laborers for his vineyard. 2 Now when he had agreed with the laborers for a denarius a day, he sent them into his vineyard. 3 And he went out about the third hour and saw others standing idle in the marketplace, 4 and said to them, 'You also go into the vineyard, and whatever is right I will give you.' So they went. 5 Again he went out about the sixth and the ninth hour, and did likewise*
*6 And about the eleventh hour he went out and found others standing idle, [a] and said to them, 'Why have you been standing here idle all day?' 7 They said to*

*him, 'Because no one hired us.' He said to them, 'You also go into the vineyard, and whatever is right you will receive.'8 "So when evening had come, the owner of the vineyard said to his steward, 'Call the laborers and give them their wages, beginning with the last to the first.' 9 And when those came who were hired about the eleventh hour, they each received a denarius. 10 But when the first came, they supposed that they would receive more; and they likewise received each a denarius.*

*11 And when they had received it, they complained against the landowner, 12 saying, 'These last men have worked only one hour, and you made them equal to us who have borne the burden and the heat of the day.' 13 But he answered one of them and said, 'Friend, I am doing you no wrong. Did you not agree with me for a denarius? 14 Take what is yours and go your way. I wish to give to this last man the same as to you. 15 Is it not lawful for me to do what I wish with my own things? Or is your eye evil because I am good?' 16 So the last will be first, and the first last. For many are called, but few chosen."*
(Matthew 20: 1-16)


## Elements of the Parable

Landowner- He went out four times. God continually seeks workers for His vineyard. Workers- they were ready to work, but... they wanted to work on their own terms and adjust the terms to suit themselves. It does not work that way. Vineyard-the work was there to be done. The vineyard is always waiting. There are different tasks, but there is always work to be done. Marketplace-Why were they there? Ever notice the men standing around waiting for work? There are places of expectation where workers congregate to be picked up for a day's work. Wages? They all received the same wages. Length of service? The time they worked was different.

**What is this about?**
The Kingdom
The King is sovereign.
He paid the price to own the vineyard.
He went outside the vineyard to find the workers.
He went four times.
He needs workers to tend the vineyard.

**The Fairness Test**
What is fair?
Is getting what is promised enough?
If one's reward is greater or less than another's, is that unfair?
What is the difference between being called and being chosen?

**The Father's Expectation**
The Father expects us to work in His vineyard. It is the mission of every believer to be a vineyard worker. Some plant, some water, some prune, some reap and some stand guard. Regardless of how long we work or when we are called, we will receive what He has promised. He expects to see fruit and to reap a crop. Each worker has a part in the harvest.

**A Fresh Baked Loaf of Bread**
A few years ago, my daughter gave us a bread machine. The bread machine is not very large and has

the capacity to do the whole job of preparing and baking the loaf. You put all the ingredients in it and you set the timer and it bakes the bread and it comes out virtually perfect every time, if you do the right things. Pretty easy because they have these bread mixes that you can buy. They're expensive, but they make a perfect loaf of bread. Just follow the simple directions. I'm an innovator, (Robert) so I like to use my own recipe. The great thing about this was, you could put all these ingredients in at night and set the machine to come on before you got up in the morning. By the time you woke up the house was filled with a wonderful aroma. When you got up and went into the kitchen, you dumped the bread out of the container. You had this nice little loaf of bread and it was all soft and crusty. Just slice and put on a little butter. I can eat the whole thing. One day I decided that I wanted to deviate from the packaged recipe and make my own. I carefully measured all the ingredients. The last thing I put in was the yeast. I set the machine to come on an hour before breakfast. Next morning when I got up, the house was filled with this wonderful aroma. I opened up the machine and I looked. Instead of a nice full container, there was only about two inches of bread in the bottom of the container. I thought, "What the heck happened here"? As I dumped it out, a sound issued forth. Thump! It was like a rock. I tried to slice it, but I could not. We tried throwing it down to break it. Our dog even refused our offer to chew on it as a dog bone. We discovered the culprit was old yeast.

The Kingdom of God is kind of like that, if you will. I mean, the aroma that you produce when you are walking in a Kingdom way, is so attractive it draws people in. It makes them hungry. The Kingdom itself is like that succulent piece of bread when it's perfectly done. It's a taste, an aroma, and an almost way of being that's delightful, if you will. But mess up the ingredients and it's not even fit for the dogs. Ouch! Our charge is that we portray the Kingdom to those outside the Kingdom, in such a way that they are attracted to God's delight.

The Kingdom is:
Taste, Smell, Texture!
Nourishing.
An experience you want!
Something to be shared.
It can be spoiled by a little error!
When spoiled, it is only good for the dogs.
It has a drawing appeal.
It produces a lasting appeal that you want to repeat.

## What Do These Parables Mean to My Life?

Am I a reluctant worker?
Am I waiting to be hired-told what to do?
What part of the market place is my vineyard?
How should I now live?

Am I out sowing seeds?
Am I preparing a place for the birds to rest?
Am I fruitful?
Do I have a drawing fragrance?

How can you fulfill your mission in your current circumstances? If your current circumstances are blockading your mission, what needs to change?

# Jesus had a mission statement.

*[1]The Spirit of the Sovereign Lord is on me,*
*because the Lord has anointed me*
*to proclaim good news to the poor.*
*He has sent me to bind up the brokenhearted,*
*to proclaim freedom for the captives*
*and release from darkness for the*
*prisoners,[a]*
*[2] to proclaim the year of the Lord's favor*
*and the day of vengeance of our God,*
*to comfort all who mourn,*
*[3] and provide for those who grieve in Zion—*
*to bestow on them a crown of beauty*
*instead of ashes,*
*the oil of joy*
*instead of mourning,*
*and a garment of praise*
*instead of a spirit of despair.* (Isaiah 61:1-3)

## The Mission of the Church

As the church, we can fulfill our Isaiah 61 mission by doing those things listed which will inject the seven mountains of cultural influence with righteousness and Kingdom principles such that we cause a Niagara of reversal, repentance, and revival that leads to reformation and transformation.

Thy Kingdom come. Thy will be done on Earth....

# PART IV

# YOUR PROVISION FOR THE FUTURE

When you are walking in your God-given mission, God obligates Himself through His covenant promise, to provide your provision.

# CHAPTER 12

# REMOVING BLOCKADES TO YOUR FUTURE

## New Thought Patterns for Securing Your Provision

Your provision for your future is tied up with your mission and destiny. This calls for a new way of thinking about finances for our future. It's time to be transformed by the renewing of our minds. It is time for applying God's principles for increase, to our finances. We are always thinking about, "Where's the next dollar coming for this thing or the other?"

God, however, has made provision for every need for our mission in life. Your provision is definitely tied to your mission. Father God planned our unique destiny before we were born. If you're moving out towards your mission, you are moving forward and you will find your provision along the pathway. By faith, it's already there. It's always been planned to be there for your assignment. The Lord wants us always moving towards our horizon, in harmony and partnership with Him. Always!

> *18 But remember the LORD your God, for it is he who gives you the ability to produce wealth, and so confirms his covenant, which he swore to your ancestors, as it is today.* (Deut. 8:18 NIV)

(We speak more in depth on this matter in Chapter 15.)

## Remember these five things

**When your mind is renewed, you are open to the thoughts God has for you.** If you are thinking about all of the bad things which have or could happen, you will not be able to receive the thoughts God has for you, as you press forward. Renewing your mind requires faith, and faith requires acting on God's Word. You apply it in order to change the way you have been thinking concerning your needs, your life, your work, and your future.

### 1. Our conscious thoughts must be clear and unfettered by disobedience and unhindered by sinful actions and addictions.

I (Annette) have a saying. "Sin makes you stupid!" When our minds are cluttered with thoughts not inspired by God, we do not see things as clearly as He intends. Too often, we make decisions out of fear instead of faith. The renewed mind is not hindered by sin, but reflects the nature of God. Sinful actions and addictions often have their source in past hurts and trauma. The addictive act releases endorphins in the brain which produce (at least temporarily) a state of wellbeing. It seems that the act medicates the hurt, but only for a moment. <u>Healing the hurt is the only way to be free of it.</u>[31]

2. **When iniquity enters into the situations and circumstances of life, it forms a blockade to your prosperity.**

Iniquity opens portals for demonic invasion and attack. It helps to form strongholds of darkness. How can we help build a fortress to combat evil if we are supplying the enemy with ammunition against the establishment and increase of the Kingdom of God? How can God bless us if we are not making choices which He can bless? God clearly covenants to be our supply but not when we are moving contrary to His instructions and boundaries. If there is a stronghold, there must be repentance and deliverance.

3. **<u>Redeem the land</u>, clear the blockades, and restore the covenant.**

Research the land. <u>Find the hidden things</u> that the people who dwelled there have done. Go to God. Confess the sin, take responsibility for it. Even make a sacrificial gift, if that is in order. Plan how to occupy the territory you have cleansed.

The Lord has been speaking to us more and more about the need for cleansing the land. He is stirred up about the unsaved in your city, your community, your church, and your home. He desires a relationship with His creation.

We will go more into the causes of the need for Redeeming the Land in a little while.

4. **Maintain the Territory.**
**Keep it cleansed and maintained. Visit the territory and establish a work there.**

Finally, the fifth thing to remember:

5. **Let faith take over!**

-----------------------

Here is what you will need to know so that the land can be redeemed.

# Seven Things Which Pollute the Land

In Ezekiel 14, we find how idolatry pollutes the land.

*[1]Some of the elders of Israel came to me and sat down in front of me. [2] Then the word of the Lord came to me: [3] 'Son of man, these men have set up idols in their hearts and put wicked stumbling-blocks before their faces. Should I let them enquire of me at all? [4] Therefore speak to them and tell them, "This is what the Sovereign Lord says: when any of the **Israelites set up idols in their hearts a**nd put a wicked stumbling-block before their faces and then go to a prophet, I the Lord will answer them myself in keeping **with their great idolatry.** [5] I will do this to recapture the hearts of the people of Israel, who have all deserted me for their idols."* [6] *'Therefore, say to the people of Israel, "This is what the Sovereign Lord says: Repent! **Turn from your idols** and renounce all your detestable practices!*

# Idolatry

**1.** Idolatry is the worship of something or someone other than God, who is the creator of heaven and earth, as if it were God.

Idolatry **curses the land** and puts a blanket or a hood over it. The people although hearing, cannot hear the gospel. You may be laying out God's good plan for them, but they don't get it or want it. Why? The land is polluted.

> *Wherefore, my dearly beloved, flee from **idolatry**.* (I Cor. 10:14 KJV)

> *Thou shalt have no other gods before me.*
> *[4] Thou shalt not make unto thee any graven image, or any likeness of anything that is in heaven above, or that is in the earth beneath, or that is in the water under the earth.[5] Thou shalt not bow down thyself to them, nor serve them.* (Exodus 20:3-5)

# The Shedding of Innocent Blood

**2.** Grief comes upon the land from the innocent blood shed because of hatred, unforgiveness, racial intolerance, injustice, and abortion to name a few of the major causes. Because of these, we should be moved to tears in our intercession. When we see whole communities with boarded up houses, we remember God's word says that "the land will vomit out its inhabitants" when the land is polluted. (Lev 18:25) We do not lay this at the feet of just those who lived out the last years on this land. No, the land has been around for thousands of years with people polluting it. When iniquities fill the cup to its fill, it reaches the final point when the "land vomits out its inhabitants."

We are reminded of such an example in the Bible. God's people of the time, the Hebrews, were living enslaved in Egypt. However, the land they were promised by God, through father Abraham, was currently inhabited by many tribes not loving and serving God. The Lord said the land had not yet reached its fullness of iniquity through which He would move to overthrow them, destroying them and giving their land to the promised sons of Abraham.

*"Know for certain that for four hundred years your descendants will be strangers in a country not their own and that they will be enslaved and mistreated there" And then, "In the fourth generation, your descendants will come back here, __for the sin of the Amorites has not yet reached its full measure.__"* (Genesis 15:13, 16 NIV)

Two years ago, we made a prayer journey over our whole state to pray **at every abortion clinic or hospital**. Hospitals denied that they performed abortions. We know from nurses working in them, that they just call it something else. In our state, late term abortions are allowed, so people travel here to have their abortions performed. It's not just the people of our state, but we encourage others who live in places where their laws protect the unborn innocents, to come shed more innocent blood on our soil.

## Broken Covenants

**3.** When we make covenants with others, such as marriage or peace treaties, we are giving our word to live up to our duties and responsibilities to others. In effect, we are invoking the commandment to love. When such covenants are broken, as agents of the Living God, we are dishonoring God Himself. We are living within a New Covenant that was ratified with the precious blood of Jesus. We have been bought with a price and given our freedom. We choose whom we will follow every day. If we love God with our whole hearts, and seek to walk with Him in building His Kingdom, then we are walking in covenant with Him and all His blessings and favor are available to us. If we live half the time for ourselves, are we covenant keepers?

# Immorality

**4.** Immoral life-styles! Can we really live with an "anything goes" society in the church? What does God say about that?

*[20] He (Jesus) went on: "What comes out of a person is what defiles them. [21] For it is from within, out of a person's heart, that evil thoughts come—**sexual immorality**, theft, murder, [22] adultery, greed, malice, deceit, lewdness, envy, slander, arrogance and folly.* (Mark 7:20-22 NIV)

*"As for the Gentile believers, we have written to them our decision that they should abstain from food sacrificed to idols, from blood, from the meat of strangled animals and from **sexual immorality**."* (Acts 21:25)

*"It is actually reported that there is **sexual immorality** among you, and of a kind that even pagans do not tolerate: A man is sleeping with his father's wife."* (1Cor. 5:1)

*"But now I am writing to you that you must not associate with anyone who claims to be a brother or sister but is **sexually immoral**."* (1Cor. 5:11)

In Chapter 18 of Leviticus, the Lord describes ten or so different forms of forbidden perverted sexual acts. Then He says:

> **24** *"Do not defile yourselves in any of these ways, because **this is how the nations** that I am going to drive out before you **became defiled**. 25 Even the land was defiled; so I punished it for its sin, and the land vomited out its inhabitants. 26 But you must keep my decrees and my laws. The native-born and the foreigners residing among you must not do any of these detestable things, 27 for all these things were done by the people who lived in the land before you, and the land became defiled. 28 And **if you defile the land,** it will vomit you out as it vomited out the nations that were before you.* (Leviticus 18:24-28)

# REMOVING BOUNDARIES

> *And He has made from one blood every nation of men to dwell on all the face of the earth, and has determined their preappointed times and the **boundaries** of their dwellings.* (Acts 17:26)

## Violation of Boundaries[32]

**5.** Boundaries exist for both defense and heritage. This can be seen in the plights of both the nation of Israel and in the plight of the Native Americans.[33]

> *I will also gather all nations, And bring them down to the Valley of Jehoshaphat; And I will enter into judgment with them there <u>On account of My people, My</u>*

*heritageIsrael,Whom they have scattered among the nations; They have also **divided up My land**.* (Joel 3:2)

*And He has made from one blood every nation of men to dwell on all the face of the earth, and has determined their preappointed times and the **boundaries** of their dwellings.* (Acts 17:26)

*Do not remove the ancient* [a]*landmark which your fathers have set.* (Proverbs 22:28)

*Also see* Deuteronomy 27:17. 19:14

**Please note** that boundaries also include the boundaries established by covenant and law. When God's boundaries are changed, replaced, or discarded there is also a defilement of the land. Again this leads to a rejection of authority which in turn leads to iniquitous behavior, the result is chaos and sorrow.

## Mission Failure

**6.** Passing through the days allotted to your life, never knowing your God-given Gift or Calling

Curses come to the land when God-given gifts are buried with the people, having never been recognized or used. This is the case when Christians are not taught that they are empowered by Holy Spirit to complete their life mission, and trained in spiritual warfare using their gifts to build the Lord's Kingdom by taking back lost ground. Having done that, they have missed out on the knowledge of how to redeem the land.

*"For we are God's handiwork, created in Christ Jesus to do good works, which <u>God prepared in advance for us to do</u>."* (Ephesians 2:10)

*But you are a chosen people, a **royal priesthood**, a holy nation, <u>God's special possession</u>, <u>that you may declare</u> the praises of him who called you out of darkness into his wonderful light.* (1 Peter 2:9)

Jesus said that now are we the light of the world. The royal priesthood is now the Melchizedek Priesthood as according to Hebrews 8:13, Jesus is now the new high-priest <u>forever</u>. No longer is the new covenant priesthood the Levitical priesthood, due to the new covenant demanding a new priesthood.

*"In that He says, 'A new covenant,' He has made **<u>the first obsolete</u>**."* (Hebrews 8:13)

*[12] For when **<u>the priesthood is changed</u>**, the law must be changed also. [13] He of whom these things are said <u>belonged to a different tribe</u>, and no one from <u>that tribe has ever served at the altar</u>.* (Hebrews 7:12)

Both men and women are priests in this new priesthood. The New Testament bears out this truth as it speaks of women prophets and teachers in the book of Acts. Early history accounts of the church speak of women apostles. The term <u>sat at the feet of</u> in the gospel, was a term meaning that the one spoken of, was a disciple.

*She had a sister called **Mary**, who **sat at** the Lord's feet listening to what he said.* (Luke 10:39)

## *We see that the Gifts of God are spoken of in three classifications:*

<u>Gifts of the Holy Spirit</u> given at the time of being baptized in the Holy Spirit – (1 Corinthians 12:8-11)

<u>Gifts (gift persons) given by Jesus</u> to the church on His ascension-(Ephesians 4:11)

<u>Gifts of the Father</u> given at birth to all-(Romans 12)

Earlier teaching on spiritual gifts has not given a full picture and explanation of the importance of understanding of these gifts. The three major mentions of these gifts in the New Testament (Romans 12, Ephesians 4:11, and I Corinthians 12,) were thought to be simply restatements of the same thing, and that we could expect to operate in any or all of the gifts as needed for ministry. We were also taught that some people were gifted with a higher concentration of a certain gift as the Spirit would will. Some points of view even went so far as to say that gifts are no longer available to the believer.

Over the last several years, we have reexamined these positions and see God's giftings in a much different light. Prompted by Holy Spirit, and thanks to recent teachings by today's Prophets, we now have quite a different view. Understanding becomes clearer as God's kairos time intersects with our chronos time, and His glory is revealed in the time of the culmination of all things.

The Gifts described in Romans 12, are gifts from the Father <u>given to all persons at birth</u>. These are your DNA, so to speak. The total of the seven gifts taken together in fullness are a description of the personality of God, Himself. Each of us has all seven to some degree. However, we have one of the seven that stands out above the others.

### The Gifts of God the Father

The gifts listed in Romans 12 are given to individuals at birth by the Father and <u>determine the personal character traits of the individual</u>. These are <u>innate,</u> (charis-in born) gifts in every person regardless of religious belief.

PROPHET – The one who feels drawn to

fixing things which are out of order

RULER/LEADER – The wise project manager

TEACHER – Seeker and giver of truth

GIVER – Manager of assets to produce wealth
   i.e. philanthropist

MERCY/ GRACE – Champion of the second chance

EXHORTER – Pushes beyond the immediate, encourager, expounder

MINISTER/SERVANT – Care giver

Thus, a person who has not been reborn is still gifted by God to be equipped for his/her life mission. He may function as a prophet or teacher in his life sensing what is coming up without clarity or knowledge of God's word. We often see this in movies or books.

## Gifts of Jesus – Ascension Gifts

The gifts in Ephesians 4:11 are **"gift persons" (doma)** given by Jesus to the Church at His ascension for the purpose of structure of the body and governing.

APOSTLES – Direct the course of the Church.

PROPHETS – Get direction from God to advise the apostle.

EVANGELISTS – Are passionate for souls and the Kingdom.

PASTORS/TEACHERS – Operate as care givers and instructors, identify, train, and release.

The purpose of these gifts is *"... the perfecting (equipping, building up) of the saints, for the work of the ministry, for the edifying of the body of Christ."*

<u>All believers</u> are to be trained for the work of ministry (not a select few) (Ephesians 4:12). These persons equip the saints to do the work of ministry. They do not do all the work of ministry. In some cases these persons can be identified early in life as supernaturally destined for God's calling to serve the body. In other instances, these persons emerge as their calling and walk in the spiritual life and ministry blossom. I believe that God would use us all in these ways if we were abiding in His plan and walking close to Him. However, most believers do not rise to this calling.

### Gifts of the Spirit

The gifts listed in I Corinthians 12 are gifts given from Holy Spirit and are given for the <u>manifestation</u> (<u>phanerosis</u>) of the Spirit. These gifts testify to the person of Jesus and edify (confirm the faith of) the body of Christ.

They manifest to indicate the presence of God and give power to the body of believers. Miracles happen through these gifts. The supernatural power of God brings these gifts to the forefront, to accompany and confirm the preaching of the word.

All believers may manifest these gifts as they are given by the Spirit. It is important that we delineate between the gifts in Ephesians (gifts given by Jesus for the administration and conduct of the Church) and those in Corinthians (gifts given by Holy Spirit for the empowerment of the believer). Simply because a person may prophesy, does not make that person fill the Ephesians gift of prophet. A caregiver may not necessarily be a Pastor. Because a person has the Roman's gift of the prophet (in his DNA), does not make him an Ephesian Prophet or signify that he will manifest the Corinthian gift of prophesy. However, a true Ephesians prophet will likely be a Roman's prophet by nature and exhibit the Corinthian gift of prophesy.

The list in 1Corinthians may not necessarily comprise the whole list of those areas in which Holy Spirit may empower the believer. Such examples are Sampson's gift of physical strength, David's gift of courage, or Elisha's gift of spiritual vision.

The list in I Corinthians 12 is as follows:

**Speaking in Tongues** – An unknown (to the speaker) language in an audible series of sounds, which may be recognizable as a spoken language by an observer. We know of many situations in which the Tongue is readably translated by someone who hears it spoken.

**Interpreting Tongues** – In this case the hearer does not know the language, but receives from Holy Spirit the meaning of the utterance.

**Word of Wisdom -** The believer receives from Holy Spirit a deep and abiding sense of the correct application of knowledge and conduct concerning a specific situation or circumstance.

**Word of Knowledge -** This is information that the believer could not know in the absence of divine inspiration.

**Faith** – While all believers have a measure of faith, Holy Spirit gives an extra strong dependence of the believer in the promises and power of God, based upon His word.

**Healing** – While Jesus gave His followers the authority to heal, Holy Spirit enhances that authority with power. The individual exhibiting this gift will often see immediate and dramatic healings occur.

**Miracles** – Again, this is an enhancement of the authority of the believer, but with dramatic and instant results. Power over the elements of weather is an example.

**Prophecy** – The person may have a clear understanding of the application of scripture to a circumstance or even a predictive insight of things to come.

**Discerning of Spirits** – Holy Spirit shows the individual the nature of cause and effect in a given situation. They would have insight as to how a spirit may gain entrance or have power in a situation. This is especially important in deliverance and may be accompanied by a sense of how to proceed.

Gifts of the Spirt are important since the mission of Jesus to His followers (including us), could not be fulfilled without these empowering attributes.

## God Robbers [34]

### 7. With-holding tithes and offerings

*"But you ask, 'How are we robbing you?'*
*"In tithes and offerings. [9]* **You are under a curse—your**
**whole nation—because you are robbing me.** *[10] Bring the*
*whole tithe into the storehouse, that there may be food in*
*my house. Test me in this," says the* LORD *Almighty, "and*
*see if I will not throw open the floodgates of heaven and*
*pour out so much blessing that there will not be room*
*enough to store it. [11] I will prevent pests from*
*devouring your crops, and the vines in your fields will not*
*drop their fruit before it is ripe," says*
*the* LORD *Almighty. [12]* **"Then all the nations will call you**
**blessed, for yours will be a delightful land**,*" says*
*the* LORD *Almighty.* (Malachi 3:8-10 )

These seven things pollute the land. All the churches who have been baptized in the Holy Spirit, having the gifts of the Holy Spirit as listed in 1 Cor. 12, should learn how to go out and pray over the land, with repentance, redeeming the land, so the gospel can be heard. Jesus can then get the full harvest for which He already has paid for in His blood.

*Those things that you neglect to deal with, will probably come back to rear their heads in the future.*

# CHAPTER 13

## FILLING THE GAP

### The G.A.P.

Most of you know that we generally center in on Romans 12:1 and 2 because that's our life scripture.

> *"I beseech you therefore, brethren, by the mercies of God, that ye present your bodies a living sacrifice, holy, acceptable unto God, which is your reasonable service. [2] And be not conformed to this world: but be ye transformed by the renewing of your mind, that ye may prove what is that good, and acceptable, and perfect, will of God."* (Romans 12: 1- 2),

You remember that God showed me good, acceptable, and perfect: **g** for good, **a** for acceptable, **p** for perfect, **G-A-P** spells gap. When you're standing in the gap, you stand taking what the situation *is* to what is God's good and acceptable and perfect will. You stand in that gap by faith. You know God's good and acceptable and perfect will because you have a renewed mind. Now you can't know God's good and acceptable and perfect will unless your mind is renewed. Getting your mind renewed is a process of filling it with God's word. As you fill your mind with God's word you learn His good and acceptable and perfect will. Then you apply that good and acceptable and perfect will to the situation. That is what you do when you pray for healing. That is what you do when you pray for any purpose. When you say, "I'm standing in the gap, now you know what you're standing in. You're standing in the absence of God's good and acceptable and perfect will. Your job is to bring His good, acceptable, and perfect will into the situation. You fill the gap with your faith, which is evidence and substance. He also showed me that wherever a gap happens, there is an opportunity, by faith, to go forth through the gap into enemy territory. As we go into enemy territory, we take back ground for the Lord. We not only have to redeem it, we have to occupy it. That's right! Then set the new horizon, by which we move forward, to take more territory.

Let us look again at Romans 12: 1 and 2 from the
Message Bible. You will find it a little differently expressed.

## Place Your Life Before God

*Here's what I want you to do, God helping you: Take your everyday, ordinary life—your sleeping, eating, going-to-work, and walking-around life—and place it before God as an offering. Embracing what God does for you is the best thing you can do for Him. Don't become so well-adjusted to your culture that you fit into it without even thinking. Instead, fix your attention on God. You'll be changed from the inside out. Readily recognize what He wants from you, and quickly respond to it. Unlike the culture around you, always dragging you down to its level of immaturity, God brings the best out of you, develops well-formed maturity in you.* (Romans 12: 1-2 MSG)

Hallelujah. That's a little different, but essentially the same words. Remember, the Message Bible was written by a pastor from Baltimore, Eugene Peterson. As I understand it, this version is not a paraphrase, it is a translation. The difference being is that he went back to the original sources and translated it into a modern form of English. What blockades that, what stops us - the blockade obviously is **fear**. Fear is the opposite of faith, is it not? You know the definition of **fear** is believing that something that hasn't happened will happen. The definition of **faith** is believing that something that hasn't happened will happen. It's the same definition. It takes as much energy to have faith as it does to have fear. So, replace your fear with faith by knowing God's word with a renewed mind that understands His good and acceptable and perfect will. Bill Johnson says this, "If you are operating in fear, worship! Worship takes you out of fear and puts you into trust." Remember, it is the nature of the human mind to be at enmity with God. I need to have my mind renewed to know God's **g**ood and **a**cceptable and **p**erfect will. That is G-A-P; GAP!

Iniquity shows up in the land. The land needs to be redeemed when there are curses caused by iniquitous activity. When the people disobey, God's wrath as expressed in His covenants is evident in the land conditions. Now listen to this clearly. *Land conditions indicate that there is a presence of iniquity that is bringing about God's wrath to fall upon the land.* God says it over and over again. When the area is filled with iniquitous activity, we can see the evidence around us. He says clearly that we need to humble ourselves, pray, seek His face, confess our (whoever's) sins, repent, and turn from our (or others) wicked ways. Then He will forgive, and restore.

### Fear, Worship, Trust

> *The nature of the human mind is that it is at enmity with God. We must be renewed to know God's Good, Acceptable, and Perfect Will. – Bill Johnson*

### All Sin Has Corporate Consequence

That's one of my razors: **All sin has corporate consequence.** There are no secret sins. God knows all of them! This is so easy to understand and yet so important- God is bound by His own covenant. When God makes a covenant with us, He's bound to perform that covenant, because He is God and He cannot lie. God says, if you do this, you will have blessing and if you do this, you will have curse. If you do the forbidden thing, the curse is going to come. It's your choice, blessing or curse. Which way do you want to go? We must cleanse the land from the curse. We must go onto the place where the curse occurs and redeem it, caste out the iniquity and reverse the whole purpose, then occupy that place. That is why we witness to people. We witness to people to get them saved. Why? Well, so they won't go to hell, but it's bigger than that. We want to change the environment. We are change agents who go out and change it from an iniquitous situation to a redeemed situation. It's our commission in Genesis 1:28. That's what Apostles do. We go out and show people how to move forward in this, because Apostles are sent out to change cultures. When cultures change to those of righteousness and justice, it is the Kingdom of God at work. The songs you sing, about justice and righteousness, will actually happen when you do the things that we're talking about, moving forward, especially, starting with Romans 12:1 and 2, renewing your mind.

Let's talk about how the land gets polluted. Look at Ezekiel. Not only does he tell us how it gets polluted, he tells us what God wants to do about it and how He goes to great length to keep from causing curse to come. Yet, when He has exercised whatever He can do and we don't do our part, curse will come. In Ezekiel 22:23-30, you'll see where God speaks about the sins of four groups of people - the prophets, the priest, the princes and the ordinary people of the land.

*And the word of the LORD came to me, saying, <sup>24</sup> "Son of man, say to her: 'You are a land that is not cleansed[a] or rained on in the day of indignation.' <sup>25</sup> (They're talking about God's indignation.) The conspiracy of her prophets in her midst is like a roaring lion tearing the prey; they have devoured people; they have taken treasure and precious things; they have made many widows in her midst. <sup>26</sup> **Her priests have violated My law** and profaned My holy things; they have not distinguished between the holy and unholy, nor have they made known the difference between the unclean and the clean; and they have hidden their eyes from My Sabbaths, so that I am profaned among them. <sup>27</sup> **Her princes in her midst** are like wolves tearing the prey, to shed blood, to destroy people, and to get dishonest gain. <sup>28</sup> **Her prophets plastered them with untempered mortar**, seeing false visions, and divining lies for them, saying, 'Thus says the Lord GOD,' when the LORD had not spoken. <sup>29</sup> The people of the land have used oppressions, committed robbery, and mistreated the poor and needy; and they **wrongfully oppress the stranger**. <sup>30</sup> So I sought for a **man among them** who would **make a wall** and **stand in the gap** before Me **on behalf of the land**, that I should not destroy it; but I found no one. "*(Ezekiel 22: 23-30)

Notice that He did not want to destroy the land, even though the people were so corrupt that they had polluted the land. However, He did not find anyone to stand in the gap and plead for the land and the people, to give them another chance.

*"Therefore I have poured out My indignation on them; I have consumed them with the fire of My*

*wrath; and I have recompensed their deeds on their own heads," says the Lord."* (Ezekiel 22:31)

## Sin Has a Trickledown Effect

Sin has a trickledown effect that clouds revelation and stymies innovation. Think of that, it stymies innovation. Remember that there's personal iniquity, and there's corporate iniquity. They both defile the land. When we go to repentance, we personally repent and we take responsibility. Then, we corporately repent as we identify with the sin of the people, who in previous times, sometimes centuries ago, lived before us on our land. This is called identificational repentance. You identify with the sins that other people have committed. When confessing these sins, we say, *"We have sinned against you, Lord".* Let me tell you, after 46 years, I've discovered it really is *we*, from God's view point.

I (Annette) tell a personal story which exemplifies identificational repentance. At early morning corporate prayer, the Lord said to me, "Stand up and confess the sin of abortion". This was when Robert and I were pastoring a church. I said, "If I do that, the church will think I'm guilty of abortion". He said, "Well, what makes you think you aren't?" Wow! That was a real "WOW" to me. You know there are sins of commission and sins of omission. I reflected on how many times I had fasted to end abortion. How many times had I really prayed every day for Him to do something about that? Or did I support with money, those who were there trying to do something about it? I saw that I was guilty. That gave me a whole perspective on all Ten Commandments and how God looks at the sin of the world.

Those who don't know, I was raised a Roman Catholic and was mostly a daily church worshipper before I became a teacher. There were some Saturdays that I did not attend but tried to make the first Saturdays of the month. I would go to confession once or twice a month and I'd reflect on the Ten Commandments and reflect what I'd done wrong. It was always the same two commandments and the other eight? "Eh?" I would just skip over those. After becoming an adult, I was still doing the same kind of thing in my mind, though no longer a Catholic. It's a very good thing to daily think about what God might be saying about us at the end of a day. Well, in a flash, Holy Spirit revealed to me, how I was breaking almost all of His Commandments, in thought if not in deed. Wow! What a different way to view all this. It's easier to say *we* have sinned against You, my God. *We* have caused this mess in our city. *We* have done this to Your land. To clarify this once again, I am saying when we are praying identificational prayers of repentance, we can say honestly, forgive ME for the part I have played in "not doing what I could have done to reverse the destroying condition. To remind you, the first mandate God gave the first man and woman, was to watch over the land, and steward it. In the 1st chapter of Genesis, at the 28th verse, God tells us to watch over the land. How are we doing on that front?

Here are three scriptures which are examples of identificational prayer for repentance that are in the Bible and they are all from the prophets.
Ezra 9:6-10, 11-15, Nehemiah 1:6 and Daniel 9:5-7

These are useful when you go out to pray over the land. Also from the New Testament:

> - *"If we say that we have no sin, we deceive ourselves, and the truth is not in us. If you confess your sins, He is faithful and just to forgive us our sins, and <u>to cleanse us from all unrighteousness</u>."* (1John 1:8 and 9)

**Iniquity - The Sin Pattern**

We think iniquity is a repeated sin pattern and that is true. But that is not all there is to it. Let me ask you a question – what would you do if you suddenly got $10,000? Maybe you came into an inheritance. With no warning, you have $10,000 and you say, "Well, what can I do with $10,000?" How many people would think of something to spend it on? Most of us would. The $10,000 would soon be gone. Is that correct? How many people would say, "How can I invest this to make more money?" It's a different mindset, isn't it? Consumers spend, but wealthy people invest. It is a godly principle and we're going to show you that through the parable of the talents. (Luke 19:11-27)

God wants you to wisely use that which He's placed in your hand. It may be to pay a bill, but it may also be to invest it wisely in something that will produce more. Wasting what God has put into your hand is really sinful. Doing it repeatedly is iniquity that defiles. If you do not learn to properly utilize your God given assets in the least situation, how can He trust you with greater? When you finish the present assignment well, you are ready to be catapulted into the next level of your mission, which always includes finances.

*As you fill your mind with God's word you learn His good and acceptable and perfect will. Then you apply that good and acceptable and perfect will to the situation.*

# CHAPTER 14

## PARABLES-HOT TOPICS OF THE DAY

### The Parable of the Talents

Conventional teaching says that parables were nice made up stories that Jesus used to demonstrate a religious point of view. That's actually not quite accurate. If you were taught that, put it aside. The stories that Jesus used were relevant, contemporary topics that were occurring in the people's lives which He adapted and used to illustrate the point. In other words, He picked hot topics out of the local news items of the day. The Lord told me a long time ago, if I wanted to witness to Jewish people, I had better know what they're talking about. The conversation in the Jewish community can be very different than that of the gentile community today. I can prove that by getting a copy of the Jewish Times and reading you the news articles. You might be amazed at what is written. The sermons by the Jewish Rabbis have little or nothing to do, in most cases, with the Bible. I began to understand Jewish thought, in the sense that, when you read what's talked about in the Jewish community, it can be a very different mindset from the gentile Christian community.

*[11] While they were listening to this, he went on to tell them a parable, because he was near Jerusalem and the people thought that the Kingdom of God was*

*going to appear at once. 12 He said: "A man of noble birth went to a distant country to have himself appointed king and then to return. 13 So he called ten of his servants and gave them ten minas.] 'Put this money to work,' he said, 'until I come back.' 14 "But his subjects hated him and sent a delegation after him to say, 'We don't want this man to be our king.'*

*15 "He was made king, however, and returned home. Then he sent for the servants to whom he had given the money, in order to find out what they had gained with it. 16 "The first one came and said, 'Sir, your mina has earned ten more.' 17 "'Well done, my good servant!' his master replied. 'Because you have been trustworthy in a very small matter, take charge of ten cities.' 18 "The second came and said, 'Sir, your mina has earned five more.' 19 "His master answered, 'You take charge of five cities.' 20 "Then another servant came and said, 'Sir, here is your mina; I have kept it laid away in a piece of cloth. 21 I was afraid of you, because you are a hard man. You take out what you did not put in and reap what you did not sow.'*

*22 "His master replied, 'I will judge you by your own words, you wicked servant! You knew, did you, that I am a hard man, taking out what I did not put in, and reaping what I did not sow? 23 Why then didn't you put my money on deposit, so that when I came back, I could have collected it with interest?'*

*24 "Then he said to those standing by, 'Take his mina away from him and give it to the one who has ten minas.'*

*25 "Sir,' they said, 'he already has ten!'*

*26 "He replied, 'I tell you that to everyone who has, more will be given, but as for the one who has nothing, even what they have will be taken away. 27 But those enemies of mine who did not want me to be king over them—bring them here and kill them in front of me. (LUKE 19: 11-27)*

## To Occupy

(1) To take & hold possession of, as by *conquest.*

(2) To busy or engage; employ.

Put to use - operate

We can see a different orientation to this scripture than I had ever seen before.

1. They thought that the Kingdom of God was soon to come.
2. He (the Nobleman) gave them each what they needed to work with.
3. He told them to "occupy till I come".

## The Kingdom

This scripture is a Kingdom scripture. It is about responsibility, accountability and authority. It speaks to us in our time and place of what is expected of a citizen of the Kingdom. How well are we rising to the task?

The Kingdom that they expected to soon come was likely very different than the Kingdom Jesus describes in the parable. He told many parables of the Kingdom. Often, they began with "the Kingdom of God is like…" You might ask the question why He spoke like this. The simple reason is that He was correcting the common misconceptions and ignorance of the Kingdom of God. I suspect that among believers today that this same set of distortions still exists. Is it, "Pie in the sky in the great by and by," "no more sorrow, no more tears, no more the abominable thing," or "a land flowing with milk and honey"? None of these are an accurate depiction of God's Kingdom!

A second thing to consider here, is that Jesus told parables. He spoke Kingdom principles using illustrations that were familiar to the people, but with veiled meanings. Many of these stories drove very salient points and some were obscure. When I was asking The Lord how to witness to Jewish people, He led me to understand that I need to know what the topics of conversation were in the Jewish community. I could do this by using the Internet and looking up the latest articles in the Jewish Times and the latest sermons by leading Rabbis. Was I in for a surprise? The topics of conversation were often very foreign from my gentile perspective and the sermons had little or nothing to do with God or the Bible. The perspective was often ethical and very liberal. As I got used to it, I was able to see how it was possible to take a hot topic and show a biblical application. It doesn't happen quickly, but I am getting the hang of it.

## Hot Topics

I am convinced that in the parables Jesus used "Hot Topic" issues that were the gossip of the market place. He linked with the common discussions of the time and gave them a Kingdom slant.

Other times, Jesus used familiar things like planting seeds or holding a candle. These were things to which the common people could relate.

**It's about the land. If the land is defiled then nothing can prosper. Redeem the land. Then pursue your prosperity.**

This particular parable in Luke 19:11-27, what we call the parable of the talents, may have come from the news of the day. It's a parallel to the story of the son of Herod, Archelaus. When Herod died, his son did not automatically receive Herod's mantle. He had to go to Rome and he had to plead his case and there were several people contending for it. He was gone for some time; it was, probably nearly a year, as travel was slow in those days. It took over 20 days to get from Jerusalem to Rome by ship. Once he got there he had to wait in line, so to speak, to plead his case. He was gone for some time. Jesus recounts that the rich young ruler, (Archelaus probably), called ten of his servants together. He gave them each a pound or a talent which was equivalent to at least a month or maybe as much as three month's wages. And he said to them, ten of them, *occupy till I come*. Now that word occupy doesn't mean - *sit on it*. It means - *put it to use, take it, and use it!* He then went off to a far country to claim his rulership. So, then it says, he came back. He returned. He interviewed three of the ten. We don't know about the other seven. He interviewed just three of the ten. The first one he interviewed had increased the talent ten times; ten times. Now if it took him a year to do that that's a thousand percent return on investment! Hello! It's pretty rare that any kind of investment produces that great a return. The second one produced five of what he was given. Again, if it took a year, five hundred percent return. That is still pretty good, right? But the third man said, "You're a tough guy. You know I'm scared of you and so I wrapped it up and sat on it. I occupied that sucker. I just sat on it and here it is back." The ruler called him <u>a wicked, faithless, servant</u>. You have the first two who are faithful and faith-filled. You have the third who is faithless. While we don't know about the other seven, we do know there was another group of people, who didn't want him to rule over them at all. They actually lobbied to keep him from getting his Kingship. When they lobbied to keep him from getting his Kingship he looked at them as enemies and it says that he called them to be destroyed ( as did Archelaus).

***If you want to see more authority in your life, then you have to be productive in another man's vineyard - Bill Johnson***

The interesting part of this is the first two servants, who were faithful, were then given authority over cities. The man who earned ten was given authority over ten cities, and not only that he was given the additional money that the third guy didn't do anything with. He not only got authority, he got additional money. The same thing is true of the second man. He got authority over five cities. The degree to which they were productive was the degree to which they were given authority. Let me say that again! If you want to see authority then you have got to be productive in another man's mission. When you're productive for someone else, you receive a natural authority, a Kingdom authority, if you will.

A good demonstration of this is the life of Daniel. I love reading Daniel. It is beneficial to study it once a year. He served three one-world rulers and he served them well. Made them prosper more than they would have if he had not been there. When one of these world rulers was getting ready to be punished by the Lord, Daniel was greatly moved in sorrow to have to tell that ruler what was going to happen. He cared for the ruler who did not know God. He was a faithful employee/steward of what was not his, but which made him prosper. When one would die and some other one came to rule next, they heard of him and had him brought in and he served them and made them prosperous. In this present time, *we need Daniels*! We need Daniels because many parts of the ruling world may not come to know the Lord, but when a child of God serves them, that nation may become a sheep nation. A sheep nation is not necessarily a Christian nation, but one where the people can live in peace while being able to live and share the saving gospel without persecution. You know we have not had much teaching on this in the Church. You probably think that you would be in your prayer closet praying against these non-Christian rulers every night. Daniel did not. He prayed three times a day, it is written. And he blessed and cursed not. That is also recorded in the New Testament in Romans 12. His life made them want to know his God. They saw how God rescued him and that he lived a virtuous life. They all knew that he was someone that could be trusted. This is no small thing. In the work place, where we are not able to speak of the Lord, our life speaks. <u>Our life speaks!</u> The contrast, between those living in darkness and the children of the light, is great! We serve a noble King and our light-filled life speaks.

Now, how does this relate to your life and to the present state of Christianity in the Church? The first book in our series called Reformation in the 21<sup>st</sup> Century Church, is called *Course Corrections*. Things we see that need to be done now. The first thing we did was to go through the book of Revelation and find the five reasons the Church would lose its lampstand. Sadly, all five reasons are present in some form in the wider body of Christ. The five things for which God said they'd lose their lampstand are present in the Church now. Does that make any sense? It would seem as if the Church today does not believe God will take away our lampstand.

Let's look at the dedication of God's temple, remembering that God is bound to His covenant. When God makes a covenant, He's going to perform it one way or the other.

## To What Do You Relate?

*12 Then the LORD appeared to Solomon by night and said to him: "I have heard your prayer and have chosen this place for Myself as a house of sacrifice. 13 When I shut up heaven and there is no rain, or command the locusts to devour the land, or send pestilence among My people, 14 if My people who are called by My name will humble themselves, and pray and seek My face, and turn from their wicked ways, then I will hear from heaven, and will forgive their sin and heal their land. 15 Now My eyes will be open and My ears attentive to prayer made in this place. 16 For now I have chosen and sanctified this house, that My name may be there forever; and My eyes and My heart will be there perpetually. 17 As for you, if you walk before Me as your father David walked, and do according to all that I have commanded you, and if you keep My statutes and My judgments, 18 then I will establish the throne of your Kingdom, as I covenanted with David your father, saying, 'You shall not fail to have a man as ruler in Israel.'*

*19 "But if you turn away and forsake My statutes and My commandments which I have set before you, and go and serve other gods, and worship them, 20 then I will uproot them from My land which I have given them; and this house which I have sanctified for My name I will cast out of My sight, and will make it a proverb and a byword among all peoples.* (2 Chronicles 7:12-20)

This is what He said to Solomon, if you go to 2 Chronicles, chapter 7, starting about the 12th verse, it says that if there is calamity on the land, If my people...pray, then He will hear...,forgive...and heal it.

Now listen, this is calamity on the land right, *if my people*, we know this scripture, <u>*if My people*</u> *who are called by My name will humble themselves, and pray and seek My face,"* humble, pray, seek His face and *turn from their wicked ways* - remember that turning, *then I will hear from heaven, will forgive their sin and heal their land.*

I want to interject that forty-eight years ago, when we were born again and filled with the Holy Spirit, we were saying, memorizing and singing that scripture just like you. Is this about who can recite it from memory? The land is not healed, so obviously one or more of these elements are missing. We can recite it! So, it's not about saying it. Are we humble?

The Lord says when those things happen (curses upon the land), then His eyes will be open and His ears attentive to prayer *made* in that place". Can we pray prayers that God doesn't hear? If we're in a place that's defiled, *"yes."* God is not going to hear the prayers that we pray from a place of defilement.

Joshua 9 is about the Gibeonites' treaty with Joshua. II Samuel 21 tells us that King David noticed after three years, that there was a drought in the land. I don't know where his mind was to take that long to respond to the drought. He asked God and God spoke right up and said that it was because of the Gibeonites and the treaty Joshua had made with them when entering Israel for the first time. David asked what it was. The Lord said that Joshua had promised to protect their lives. Actually, they were supposed to all be destroyed, but they had put on costumes to make themselves look as if they had traveled from a far-away land. They came in and Joshua was taken in by their disguises. He was Israel's leader as the one placed in authority by Moses. Therefore, whatever he said was the last word. Although he promised, many of the Gibeonites were later slaughtered by King Saul during his reign. Their blood was crying out from the land for justice. Therefore, God said, in 2 Chronicles 7:14, "when I shut up the heaven and there is no rain, then if my people will come and say this, I'll heal the land. David asked what he must do. God said that he had to ask the Gibeonites what they required. It required the blood of seven of King Saul's descendants to make this right. It was a very hard thing to do, but King David did it.

Then it says at the end of 2 Samuel 21:14, "*after that, God heard their prayers*." They had to *do something* besides just "say." That's why we're saying that what is being taught here is very noteworthy for us for today and the condition of our land.

*For now I have chosen and sanctified this house, that My name may be there forever; and My eyes and My heart will be there perpetually.* (See, that's God intent.) *[17] As for you, if you walk before Me as your father David walked, and do according to all that I have commanded you, and if you keep My statutes and My judgments, [18] then I will establish the throne of your Kingdom, as I covenanted with David your father, saying, 'You shall not fail to have a man as ruler in Israel.' [19] "But if you turn away and forsake My statutes and My commandments which I have set before you, and go and serve other gods, and worship them, [20] then I will uproot them from My land which I have given them; and this house which I have sanctified for My name I will cast out of My sight, and will make it a proverb and a byword among all peoples.* (2 Chronicles 7:16-20)

In other words, God gave every possibility to maintain the blessing that was upon Israel and upon the Temple. He said, if these other things enter in, that's it! Did God allow the Temple to be destroyed – yes! Did the Israelites rebuild it – yes! Did He allow it to be destroyed again– yes! Why, because it was no longer the place that He had sanctified. I ask you this question, why did we continue to rebuild inferior copies of the Temple in New Testament Christianity? Nonetheless, what we see here is God being faithful to His covenant. In other words, if iniquitous things come into play and the land comes under curse, then God is bound to take action. He's bound to do the things that He said He was going to do. But He will also cleanse the land, if we confess the sins of the land and our own.

Now here's the great hope in all of this. First of all, God doesn't want us to be under a curse. He will do everything He can possibly do to not destroy or curse the land and us. **The whole structure of the scriptures is about our relationship to God.** That is what the scriptures are all about. That's why we have rules. God is the Creator and He knows better how we should live than we do. He gives us the law, not because He's a stern Father, but because these are the things that are good for us. If we will live His way, we'll be blessed. That's already set into motion. If we fail to live His way, then we'll be cursed. It seems so simplistic to say that, doesn't it, but that's what it's all about. The whole rest of scripture is about God striving with man to show man that very simple principle. Jesus died to redeem us from our trespasses, so that we could return to covenantal status with God and see His Kingdom come. It wasn't that God wanted Jesus to die, it was that Jesus had to die to break the sin curse that was upon us. But the whole scripture is not about Jesus dying, it's about God's benevolence towards us to bring us back into right relationship. God says, I will give you a new covenant, I'll write the laws on your mind and your heart. Now how's He going to do that unless we're free from sin and we get a renewed mind? And when that happens, then we know God's **g**ood and **a**cceptable and **p**erfect will.

Think of it this way; God gave us His commandments as the boundaries of our relationship with Him. He wants relationship with us. A relationship without rules cannot last. In the same way, rules without relationship <u>will be broken</u>. We cannot possibly keep the commandments unless we have the relationship God intended. If we are always at the edge of the boundaries, sooner or later we will cross over into no man's land. To use a metaphor – a prize fighter who is constantly on the ropes will not likely win the fight, but a fighter who takes command of the center of the ring, will probably be the victor. God did not mean for us to be always only obeying the letter of the law. Jesus made it clear that even having perverse thoughts was as dangerous as the act itself.

They asked Jesus, "Well Lord, what do you say the greatest commandment is?" Their thinking was ("What is the greatest boundary that God has set for us"?) Of course, they were trying to trick Him. Remember what He said? He recited to them the *Shema Yisrael*; *"The Lord our God is One. You shall love the Lord your God with all your heart, with all your soul, and with all your strength"*.   Then it follows that God will honor His covenant, forgiving our sins, and healing our land…(II Chronicles 7:14)

# CHAPTER 15

# EFFECTS OF REVERSING THE REVERSAL

## The First and Greatest Commandment

> *"Hear, O Israel: The LORD our God, the LORD is one!*
> [b] *5 You shall love the LORD our God with all your
> heart, with all your soul, and with all your strength.*
> (Deuteronomy 6:4-5) *4 Then He said, "The second is
> like unto it. You shall love your neighbor as yourself"*
> (Lev. 19:18)

Note that He did not say it was the same, but rather like unto
it.

## The Effect of Reversal

Now, pause a minute. What happens when we
reverse the first and the second commandment that
Jesus gave? If we put loving man first **before** loving
God, what happens? We start looking at the concerns
of men and we begin to view God through man's eyes
rather than viewing man through God's eyes. We turn
things upside down. And the resultant thing is that we
reject authority, we open the door for **humanism**. We
open the door for what we call **post-modern
thinking**. Post-modern thinking means everything is
relative. Everything is not relative! Not only do we
reject ultimate authority, but the next thing we have
liberalism penetrating the Church. This leads to
liberal theology and liberation theology. We received
an email from a pastor. We weren't sure what the

pastor meant. It seemed he was disagreeing with a position we had taken on a situation that clearly violated scriptural principles. So we called him. After we explained to him why we were calling him, he said, "Oh, I see, you put your doctrine before your praxis." I thought what in the world is he talking about? Praxis. I looked it up.[35] I didn't even know what that word praxis meant. Well, praxis is a fancy way of saying how you do things, how you practice. It's a term that's used in **liberation theology.** What he was saying to us was that human concerns are more important than what you believe. That has permeated the Church. Why do we have all these humanistic things going on that violate scripture? Unfortunately, a large portion of the church believes that way. All this wrong thinking infiltrates society; especially our schools. We cannot say a prayer in school because it might offend someone, but your children can be taught a way of life that turns them against you. Hyper liberal thinking results in a rejection of external authority. This leads to anarchy and chaos. Anarchy always leads to a new harsh form of repressive government that is stricter than the earlier form it replaces.

## God's Remedy for Chaos

God gave us the scriptures so that we would have a clear picture of our relationship with Him through His eyes and be able to relate to our fellowman. This is the basis for understanding God's Kingdom.

Within His Kingdom each of us has a unique mission. Our mission is directly related to our unique set of gifts that God puts within us. He tells us that he has a plan for our life, a plan for a hope and a future.[36] Our task is to discover that mission and then pursue it to the exclusion of any other. Knowing your mission allows you to be single minded and avoid rabbit trails even if they are of good intent. However good a task may be, it may not be the best task for you. Know when to say, "No."

## Then It Follows That God Will Honor His Covenant.

When we are pursuing our God given task, we can be assured that God will, by covenant, supply what is necessary for its completion.

> *"And you shall remember the LORD your God, for it is He who gives you power to get wealth, that He may establish **His covenant** which He swore to your fathers, as it is this day.* (Deuteronomy 8:18)

We've established the premise that God honors His covenant. Therefore, the power to get wealth is within the covenant and God is bound to His covenant. Thus when you are in the right pattern and the right standing with God, He gives you the power to get wealth. At the very least, that means the power to get that which you need to accomplish your mission. To be able to multiply what He's given you, the talents He's given you, and turn it into money and favor to do the things you need to do plus your other needs. Wealth indicates more than just enough. It is an abundance or a plentiful supply.

God opens the door for prosperity. This year there will be open doors for you. How will you know which door to pass through? Not every open door is for you to go through. Some doors may look like they are closed. The enemy does not want you to enter your future and does want you to enter into a false situation. When you know your mission, you can discern the right doors.

This is where we come back to what we have stressed for the last several years; knowing your mission.
You can know your personal mission statement for life! You can take into consideration your giftings, those things which you care about and desire to do. You can place them into a statement of one short sentence that you can recite.

Ours is plastered on the wall over our computers, at the doorway, and we recite our mission statement to ourselves regularly. It is fairly easy. Once you do that, you can walk up to an open door and say, "Where does this door lead?" If it leads you in a way that's not part of your mission, however good that leading might be, it's not for you to go through it, because going through it, will divert you from your mission. It's going to take your energy and sap your ability to do the thing that you are called to do. If you're a multi-talented person, it's very hard to turn it all towards the thing that you should be doing, that you've decided that you want to do, and to move in that way. When you take all of your forces and put them in one direction, it's like a laser-beam. They use laser beams for surgery now, without using scalpels. The laser cuts through. Remember, the enemy *doesn't* want you to go through the right door and *does* want you to go through the wrong door. It doesn't have to be a sinful door, just not a good one for you. On the other side of the door that God wants you to go through, is where your future provision lies; it's on that pathway. You are going to get discouraged if you go through a wrong door and God doesn't want us to be discouraged.

## Veil of Inconvenience

Difficulties don't stop a process – press through!

> "Stir up the faith within you to get the unlocking of revelation. Don't feed that which robs your faith, like money, fear, anxiety, and worry. Put trust in something else. In all your ways acknowledge Him. Disruptions cause fear to take over producing emotional instability. God is the creator of our emotions and He is emotionally stable. We were not meant to be in turmoil. Rest, trust in Him."
> *Bill Johnson*

Watch for what is known as *the veil of inconvenience*. What do inconveniences do? They drop a curtain in front of you and say, "Oh, you can't get through here". But in faith, we can part that curtain. If you are on your mission, believing God, and seeking His direction, your faith comes forth. You can sweep that curtain away. Whatever circumstances you find yourself in, you can go back to what is God's covenant with you. In terms of the mission He's placed in you, and the direction that He's given your life, you can push through those circumstances. Our mission is to prepare people to proclaim and demonstrate the Kingdom. It's that simple. However, that covers what we do.

God is the Creator of our emotions and God is emotionally stable. At the end of an email from us you will find a scripture:

> **Trust in the LORD** with all your heart, and lean not on your own understanding; **In** all your ways acknowledge Him, And **He shall direct** your paths. (Proverbs 3:5-6)

## A Prayer of Trust

Lord, I want to know you in my emotions, my finances, my relationships, my work, my marriage, my play, my going out and my coming ins, my ideas so I can run with them. Father God, You provide and You sustain. You give the seed for my investment and

You reward my faithfulness with authority over situations and circumstances. You are the source and sustainer of life. You are the sustainer of my economic and physical wellbeing. I worship and thank you. Amen

So, what happens? A principle you need to understand is that God throughout the scriptures, always worked **to restore** Israel to their inheritance. He always will work with you **to restore** you to your inheritance. If God said you can do it, you can do it. If God said you can have it, you can have it. I'm not saying it won't take some work and some sweat. Have faith that God will always fulfill His promises. It's not a giveaway program, you will have to strive to see it mature. You have to work your mission statement. But, when you do, He will.

I read this somewhere recently. "Just when you think you have screwed up things so badly that you have ruined Gods plan, guess again. You are not that powerful."

## Release the Glory and Unlock Our Land

When we move with new generosity, it will release the power for our breakthrough. Concentrate on the release, supply, and provision for your future. Ask the Lord to reveal to you the provision that He's already made for you along your path forward in your mission calling. Decree that no matter the troubles you've gone through, God is actually

working everything out to your good. Decree it!
**Father, you're working everything to my good!**

In the story of Joseph, remember that Joseph was in servitude in Egypt for 15 years while God was releasing provision for all of Israel. That's a pretty amazing thing. He was suffering, but God was releasing provision through that. In reading Deuteronomy 8:18, (provision to get wealth), remember the Lord your God and ask Him to give you a strategy to possess your land and He will give you the power to get wealth, **so that He may establish His covenant with you.** Remember, that power is vigor. That's what power is, it means vigor, strength, force, and capacity. God can unlock innate abilities within you to gain wealth. You may not be aware of having some of these abilities, but God can unlock them and bring forth prosperity and provision for your mission.

Abraham's son, Joseph, was going through terrible day-by-day times. People were lying about him. He got thrown into prison and kept there. He was first thrown into the pit, his brothers turned against him, sold him into slavery in a foreign nation where he did not see his father each night. Fifteen years he prospered in captivity. It doesn't say that he had any "oh me, oh my" pity parties. We know how tempting that would have been, or at least to have thought about it and wonder why everyone else was getting blessed and he was not.

Throughout scripture, we are encouraged to give thanks in the midst of our situations. This will show our faith in God that there is a reason for what is happening and God is going to bring us through the valley of destruction, through the valley of tears, through the valley of oppression and desperation---through it. You are not staying down there and building yourself a house. You are going to move through it! When you start giving God thanks, it shows Him what a person of faith you are, and faith is growing. The kind of faith that it takes that He knows you must have in the place where He is developing you for and sending you into. You have to have that kind of authority to rule over the new place and its circumstances where He's next placing you. It's amazing. He's our amazing God, amazing God!

15 years! Not 15 minutes or 15 days, and not 15 months, but **15 years!** Tell yourself this, and believe it! You are moving through your circumstances and no matter what, God is on your side. He wants you to prosper, so just imagine what He's got planned as you come through. You are coming through!

Faith investigates what Holy Spirit reveals to you. Stir up the faith within you and get revelation. He will begin to expand your thinking. You will begin getting creative ideas. He makes what was crooked straight. It takes us into our inheritance.

**It's the shortcut to breakthrough!** He will make your path straight and take you into your promised land.

*You have been chosen and equipped by God for a unique mission. Discover your intended destiny and go forth in His power and strength.*

## Prophetic word from Chuck Pierce -

Step into My timing and you'll break through right, left and frontwards, and I will be your rearguard. There's grace in My pace. Don't try to slow down, don't try to go ahead. Stay in My pace. There's fire in your fingertips! I have anointed you to send forth My Resurrection Power to release My fire and consume the rubble. Get ready, as you shoot fire from your fingertips this week, rubble will be consumed and souls will be set free." – Chuck Pierce[37]

## Books Available from Revelation 22 Ministries, Inc.

Stagmer, Dr. Robert and Annette.

_____ *Reformation in the 21st Century Church,*
    *Volume1, Course Corrections,* Baltimore MD, Amazon,
    2019

_____*Reformation in the 21st Century Church,*
    *Volume 2 Miracles, Signs, and Wonders:*
    *Part 1 The Nature of God*
    *Part 2 Biblical Foundations*
    *Part 3 Historical Foundations*
    . Lutherville, MD: Minuteman Press, 2015.

_____*Reformation in the 21st Century Church,*
    *Volume III - Go Beyond the Gap to Victory.* Lutherville, MD:
    Minuteman Press, 2016.

_____*Reformation in the 21st Century Church,*
    *Volume IV—Spiritual Warfare.* Baltimore, MD: Minuteman
    Press, 2011.

_____*Reformation in the 21st Century Church,*
    *Volume V—Are You Prepared?* Baltimore, MD:
    Minuteman Press, 2016.

_____*Transformed: A Fresh Look at Romans 12.* Conshohocken,
    PA: Infinity Publishing, 2011.

_____ *Miracles Never Cease,* Baltimore, MD, Amazon, 2019.

_____ *The Mystery of the Shofar,* Baltimore, MD: Minuteman
    Press, 2012

_____*Disconnect, Reversal, and Restoration,* Baltimore, MD,
    Amazon, 2019.

To Order Go to www.Revelation22.net
    Also available on www.Amazon.com/books (in the search
    block type Stagmer)

# PERSONAL NOTES

# PERSONAL NOTES

# END NOTES

[i] The Walters are authors of numerous books. The principles in the very popular, *Name Your Gates and Take Back Your Cities* has been applied world wide.

[2] Tim Catchim and Allen Hirsch, *The Permanent Revolution-Apostolic Imagination and Practice for the 21st Century Church,* San Francisco, Jossey-Bass 2012

[3] Luke 18:8

[4] 1John 3:8

[5] 1 Cor. 13:12, 9

[6] Jeremiah 31:31

[7] Faisal Malick, "The Political Spirit", Destiny Image Publishing (Shippensburg PA) 2008

[8] https://en.wikipedia.org/wiki/Wesleyan_Quadrilateral accessed, 12/15/2018

[9] See Revelation 2:6,15

[10] Ephesians 4:11-13

[11] Revelation 2:15-16

[12] Jon Ruthven, "What's Wrong with Protestant Theology?" and "On the Cessation of the Charismata", Word and Spirit Press (Tulsa, OK) 2011.

[13] Putting things in right order- John was of the priestly order of Aaron, His future was to be a Priest but he instead broke with the Levitical order and through the act of baptism (mikvah) of Jesus ushered in the order of Melchezidek.

[14] Jon Ruthven, "On the Quest for Authentic Theology: Protestant Tradition and the Mission of Jesus."

[15] In the meantime, Nazism and the brutalities of totalitarianism came on the scene with the Jewish holocaust. Then World War II and its aftermath Communism seemed to conquer half the world; slaughtering and enslaving millions, all supposedly in the cause of the "equitable distribution of the means of life." https://www.icr.org/article/evolving-humanist-manifestos/ Accessed 5/22/2-19

[16] For example: Marxist communism while not exactly benign, was nowhere near the brutal interpretations of Lenin, Stalin or Mao. See Marxism and Violence, https://www.jstor.org/stable/2708729?seq=1#page_scan_tab_contents Accessed July 17,2019

[17] **1 Kings 18:21**
>
> And Elijah came to all the people, and said, "How long will you falter between **two opinions**? If the Lord *is* God, follow Him; but if Baal, follow him." But the people answered him not a word.

[18] **Psalm 119:156** Great *are* Your **tender mercies**, O Lord; revive me according to Your judgments.
> **Psalm 145:9** The Lord *is* good to all, and His **tender mercies** *are* over all His works.

[19] Isaiah 58

[20] Amos 6

[21] Psalm 89:14

[22] For a further discussion of the Melchizedek Priesthood see Dr. Robert and Annette Stagmer, *Reformation in the 21st Century Church, Volume I, Course Corrections, Chapter 4,* Understanding the Melchizedek Priesthood, Revelation 22 Ministries, Inc., (Baltimore Md.) 2016
> P 33-43.

[23] UPCOUNSEL, *Difference Between Contract and Covenant.* https://www.upcounsel.com/difference-between-covenant-and-contract, accessed 9/1/2018

[24] See *Robert's Razors in Reformation in the 21st Century Church,*

[25] Jeremiah 29:11

[26] https://www.paroles-musique.com/eng/Ron_Kenoly-Righteousness_Peace_and_Joy-lyrics,p01647597, accessed 7/26/2018.

[27] Romans 4:3, Galatians 3:6

[28] Shawn Bolz, *Translating God,*

[29] Resurrection to ascension 40 days, ascension to Pentecost 10 days=50 days from resurrection to Pentecost.

[30] Tommy Reid, *Radical Revolution,*

[31] For more on this see Dr. Michael Hutchings writings on PTSD. www.globalawakening.org/PTSD

[32] Numbers 5 & 6 were identified by Apostle Chief Neigel Bigpond in an address at Church on the Rock, Oklahoma City OK October 2018.

[33] Dr. Neigel Bigpond, in an address at HAPN Conference, Oklahoma City, OK, October, 2018.

[34] Thus defilement of the land was prophetically stated by Apostle Chuck Pierce, in an internet posting in 2019.

[35] prax·is ˈpraksəs/ *noun formal*
> Practice, as distinguished from theory. "The gap between theory and praxis, text and world, Accepted practice or custom. "patterns of Christian praxis in church and society"

https://www.google.com/search?q=praxis+definition&rlz=1C1KUB
R_enUS753US753&oq=praxis&aqs=chrome.3.69i57j0l5.8702j0j7
&sourceid=chrome&ie=UTF-8 Accessed 9/20/2018

[36] Jeremiah 31:31

[37] Dr. Chuck Pierce, Breakthrough Revelation Service, Glory of Zion, Corinth TX, June 23, 2019.

Made in the USA
Middletown, DE
01 September 2019